AMONG FRIENDS:
TRAVELS IN CUBA

HEATHER MURRAY

Among Friends: Travels In Cuba
Copyright © 2016 Heather Murray All rights reserved.
First Print Edition: August 2016

Formatting: Streetlight Graphics

ISBN 978-3-033-05766-1 (paperback)
ISBN 978-3-033- 05765-4 (ebook)

An album of accompanying photos is available on:
www.travelsincuba.weebly.com

For Julian and my mother,
without whom this book would not have been written

**Nam et secundas res splendidiores facit amicitia
et adversas partiens communicansque leviores.**

For friendship makes happiness brighter and
lessens adversity by dividing and sharing it.

—*M. Tullius Cicero, Laelius De Amicitia*

CONTENTS

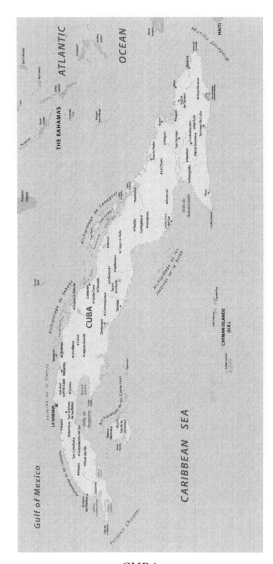

CUBA

PREFACE

MY INTENTION IN WRITING THIS book has always been to share my impressions of Cuba with travelers looking for more than gorgeous beaches, perfect weather, cheap rum and salsa lessons. Cuba's beaches and weather are great, but there's so much more to experience by getting to know ordinary Cubans outside the tourist ghettos. In fact, when I was trying to come up with a title for this book, one of the final six was *Far From The Tanning Crowd.*

This book is for those interested in what Cuba is like behind the tourist perimeter, away from the luxury resorts – and especially what life is like for Cubans. I wouldn't have been able to explore that side of Cuba without the help of Cuban friends, which is the reason for the book's title. Therefore, *Among Friends* doesn't tell you where to go or give you advice on where to stay or what to do, but I hope it does encourage you to escape from the beach resorts, strike out on your own, make contact with Cubans, stay at *hostals* and *casas particulares* and see the

1

less-traveled parts of the country on your own. You will be rewarded.

When I traveled to Cuba for the first time in December 2008, I only had a vague idea of what to expect: dilapidated buildings, old American cars and a population worn down by deprivation and resentment. This picture was challenged from the very first day. Yes, buildings in Havana were gray, but they were also ochre and red, green and light blue. Yes, people were worn down by trying to buy basic necessities with sub-standard earnings, but they were also fair and funny, smart and determined – and above all proud of their Cuban culture and identity.

That first trip was the beginning of a new love. Like Alexander von Humboldt 200 years earlier, I knew that Cuba would always occupy a place in my heart. The immediate empathy that I felt has a number of reasons. The people, first of all, are so admirably resourceful and resilient. Havana is elegant and culturally exciting, yet feels local and personal in its labyrinthine neighborhoods. There's so much history there, from the colonial mansions, convents, and fortresses to the more recent importance of the Hotel Nacional and the Museum of the Revolution. And then, when I traveled outside the capital, I realized that, besides the beaches so beloved by tourists, besides the quaint colonial towns that are accessible on guided bus tours, Cuba has inland areas of spectacular natural beauty, with rich wildlife and unspoiled ecosystems. Interested readers can see photos of some of the people

I met and the places I visited over the years on a website dedicated to my travels in Cuba, namely:

www.travelsincuba.weebly.com

This book traces my experiences in Cuba from my first trip in December 2008 to my latest visit in March 2015. It thus describes where I went, what I saw and the people I met. In addition, it covers the changes that have occurred in Cuban life since Fidel Castro handed over the presidency to his younger brother Raul. My Cuban host, Julian, who patiently explained Cuban history, etiquette, behavior, economics, education and healthcare, was also indefatigable in pointing out major changes taking place in opportunities for work, income, mobility and leisure activities. Other Cubans contributed as well, telling me personal stories about what life was like before the revolution, during the revolution and during the "special period in a time of peace" in the 1990s.

Has much changed in the eight years covered by this book? It definitely has, although visitors to the tourist resorts may not notice. For Cubans, hardships have diminished, communication with the rest of the world has blossomed and a new atmosphere of expectation has grown up. The changes have come from openings both inside and outside Cuba, and, as always, people develop skills and strategies to benefit from new opportunities. I have used the stories of the people I got to know to paint a picture of what these changes mean from a Cuban standpoint.

Finally, I'd like to express the hope that this book is as

entertaining as it is instructive. I have a strong preference for humor and adventure in travel writing, and have spent many golden hours reading and re-reading books by Gerald Durrell, Eric Newby and Bill Bryson. I would not, however, want to claim further parallels between their writing and mine.

Zurich, August 2016
Heather Murray

1
WHY CUBA?

HAVANA AIRPORT, AND I'M GOING through customs. Two inspectors heave my old black suitcase onto a white table that is floodlit by spotlights. They're wearing military caps with huge, patent leather brims and olive-colored uniforms made out of burlap. They ask, without smiling, if it's my suitcase. I nod. They unzip it and my pajamas appear, lying innocently on top of my clothes. One of the two digs deep and comes up with hi-tech earphones attached to long wires that he pulls out and winds on his arm, length after length. "That's not mine," I protest in a squeaky voice, gripped by sudden terror. "I don't know how it got there." They ignore me, intent on their search. The second inspector fishes under the neatly folded clothes and comes up with a paperback I've never seen before either. Its title is The Truth About Castro. A wailing alarm goes off at the door, as running footsteps approach…

I surface from the nightmare in full sweat as the announcement that we're landing crackles through the cabin. Outside the plane window there's only darkness. Are we still over the Atlantic? The engine softens to a whisper and we swoop lower. No, it's land. We're gliding over a velvety black land mass. Tiny pinpoints of light mark isolated dwellings, but soon organize themselves along straight lines. They must be streetlights lining a highway into Havana. There are no bright lights at all; no brightly lit sports fields, no illuminated intersections.

What am I doing, flying to a place as dark as this? It all seemed so cheerful and adventurous when I was planning the trip, but now that I'm almost there, worries start flooding my mind. What if Julian isn't at Arrivals waiting for me? He knows the address of where I'm supposed to be staying, but I don't. What if I have to take a taxi on my own? And even if I do make it to Havana alone, where should I start looking for a place to stay at nine in the evening? With each drop in altitude my adventurous mood shrivels.

This worry is ridiculous. I know Julian is absolutely dependable; he'll be waiting at Arrivals for sure. And besides, this deep darkness spread over the island is exactly what I was curious about when I first wrote to him.

That was back in 2006, when I came across a magazine article about English teaching in Cuba written by a Cuban professor. The magazine editor had written, with some condescension, that the article had been "received by post, typed on an aged typewriter" and that the author did not have an email address. These details immediately grabbed my interest. I felt a kind of tender curiosity about anyone who typed and mailed articles in this day of computer-based communication. Not only that – the author and I actually had a lot in common. We both taught English to academic professionals: Julian taught medical English to Cuban medical students and doctors, and I taught scientific English to Swiss researchers.

I wanted to write to him, but only had his name – Julian Rodriguez – and the name of his university. I wrote anyway, doubting I'd get an answer. Three months later an email from Cuba popped up in my inbox. It was from a colleague of Julian's, informing me that Julian had mailed me an answer. My letter had taken nearly three months to reach Julian, mostly due to Cuban postal problems, but also because there were two medical universities in the city where he lived. My curiosity intensified: two medical schools in the same place? According to the western press, Cuba would be lucky to have three universities in the whole country. Wasn't it a poor, run-down place, suffering through the aftermath of a failed socialist revolution and the ongoing US embargo against all things Cuban? Weren't people desperately poor?

So Julian and I started corresponding by snail mail, each letter taking about six weeks to arrive. His letters were hand-written and at first only described his work as a professor of medical English, which, after all, was what I had originally asked him about. I was surprised to discover that his teaching methods were not only modern, but in some ways more advanced than ours in Switzerland. He was, for example, allowed to enter teaching hospitals with his English classes, and could accompany student clinicians on their rounds, during which they discussed their patients in English.

After a short time we tried exchanging emails, with Julian using other people's email accounts because he didn't have one of his own. Home computers were non-existent in Cuba and some limited internet access was only available at universities. This arrangement proved to be less than ideal, however, as there was often trouble with computer access. Julian wrote:

> …Here we have lots of difficulties for communication: shortage of computers, technical problems, etc.… As you can see, we face lots of material difficulties, but we fight hard to overcome them. As you know, life is not a bed of roses, so we have to struggle to attain our goals.

Julian also kept writing paper-and-pen letters, and I reverted to that method, too. It was good to read someone's handwriting for a change. Our letters soon altered their focus; we told each other what we believed, what we liked and how we spent our free time. I wrote about my research on how English was changing Swiss communication, about visiting my family in Canada or about hiking and biking around Europe with Helga, my flat-mate and companion. In contrast, Julian wrote:

> …now I'm at the halfway stage of my summer vacation. I've spent most of the time reading, watching TV, writing, visiting friends. Traveling to other places is very difficult here, because of the shortage of transportation, so it's much better simply to stay at home, resting.… I think that Cuba is an interesting country

because it is like a sort of museum, where you can see many things that belong to a past that was overcome in Europe a long time ago. Good things and bad things, light and shadows, and many contrasts and paradoxes...

From his letters I gradually pieced together a picture of Julian, the man. He was in his mid-sixties, married and living in a small house with four other people: his wife, his mother, his grown-up son and his daughter-in-law. He was active in a local Protestant church, where he taught a Bible class for adults. He also did the English-Spanish interpreting when representatives from North-American or German churches came to visit. Not only did he not have email, he had no telephone either, relying on next-door neighbors to let him use their phone when he needed one. This, he explained, was because new telephone lines were virtually impossible to get in Cuba.

Julian taught English full-time to medical students, earning the standard salary for professional Cuban state employees of $24 per month. This was – mysteriously – enough to live on in Cuba, where food, utilities, healthcare, housing, entertainment and transport were heavily subsidized. I was fascinated. How could food, utilities and healthcare for at least three people cost less than $24 a month? Yet it did. However, if his mother needed special medications, that cost extra. Or if they wanted apples to eat at Christmas, that cost extra, too.

Within a few months of our first email exchange, Julian was able to give me the name of a Swiss man living near Zurich, who was traveling to Cuba regularly to see his Cuban fiancée. I was told that this man might take letters and other things to Julian for me. Thus it was that I met Cyril, a kind and willing Swiss theology student, whom I loaded down with English-Spanish medical dictionaries and, later, my old laptop to take to Cuba. He very obligingly did this several times, thereby saving me a great deal of money in customs duty and postage. More than that, by taking the books and computer in his luggage, Cyril ensured that the things actually reached Julian intact, which I'd heard was often not the case with mailed parcels. Julian had not asked me to send specific items, but I was very happy to be able to do something useful for a colleague – someone who was more or less doing the same job I was, but who happened to be doing it in less favorable circumstances.

Corresponding with Julian – whose name, Cyril informed me, was pronounced "Hooli *AHN*" – helped me picture daily life in Cuba. I was curious to find out how things worked in a country where goods and services were shared "from each according to his ability to each according to his need". I'd often read that Castro's revolution had achieved far less than it had promised. But how fair and how open was Cuban society? Were Cubans "brainwashed" or coerced in some way to support the Castro regime? Were our letters and emails read by someone working for the government? How did Cubans view the rest of the world? The more I thought about it, the more I wanted to observe life in one of the last socialist countries for myself.

Even though I'm Canadian on paper, I've always

loved living in Europe. I moved to Switzerland in 1970, three years after graduating from Harvard. At that time, Europe was still divided by the Iron Curtain, and I made a point of traveling to socialist countries like Romania and Yugoslavia because I was curious about how people lived there. I found that living conditions were a bit spartan and drab in terms of consumer goods, but those things didn't seem to prevent people from living healthy, fulfilling lives.

Part of my curiosity about Cuba stemmed from the time just before I moved to Europe, when I'd worked for a major publisher – Macmillan – in New York City. There I was promptly recruited into the US Socialist Workers Party by my managing editor. Weekly meetings took place in an old brick warehouse in lower Manhattan, where we used to sit in a circle arguing about ways to end the war in Vietnam. When we weren't planning protests, we heard all about Cuba and the accomplishments and bravery of Castro's revolution – the absence of economic class, the self-sacrifice of heroes like Che Guevara, the volunteers that were sent to help third-world countries. Cuba was something positive – a beacon of hope compared to the lies and mess and slaughter connected with the war in Vietnam.

Now, nearly forty years on, when Julian's letters described what life was like in present-day Cuba, I was reminded of everything I'd seen, heard and read about socialist societies. I wanted to see Cuba for myself. And Julian encouraged me to come to Cuba too; he'd already invited me to attend a number of academic conferences there.

I knew that Cuba was cut off from world trade by the US embargo, which had been imposed after Cuban nationalization of American businesses in 1960, and particularly after the "Cuban missile crisis" of 1962. For the same reasons, the United States didn't allow its citizens to travel to Cuba directly. I had a Canadian passport, however, and could fly there from Europe relatively easily. The only snag was that Cuba required individual visitors to have some kind of visa stating the purpose of their trip. If I wanted to visit Julian and see Cuba as a private tourist, I would need a visa, too.

Finally, in 2008, after two years of slow correspondence, an opportunity to get a visa, visit Cuba and meet Julian presented itself. Julian had several times mentioned that ANGLO, an English teachers' association, held a conference in Havana every December. He encouraged me to be a conference speaker, so I sent an email to the association secretary, applying to give a poster presentation. My idea was to use a talk I'd already prepared, and present it to a small group of English teachers in some quiet corner of the university, assuring myself a low-stress conference. I would get an official invitation to Cuba from the ANGLO organizers, which would guarantee me an entry visa, and thus I would also get to meet Julian and experience life in post-revolutionary Cuba. A perfect solution.

I submitted my proposal for a twenty-minute presentation to the ANGLO email address. Remarkably soon thereafter, I was notified that my proposal had been accepted: I was invited to travel to Havana at my own expense.

The real surprise came some weeks later, when I was sent the conference program. There were no poster presentations listed; instead, I was featured as one of three main speakers. Not only that, but I was scheduled to address the full membership of ANGLO at a conference to be held in a building called the Capitolio, located in the center of Havana. Not exactly a low-stress talk in some obscure university hallway.

The next thing was to get my visa or "tourist card" from the Cuban consulate in Bern. I'd been told on the phone that I'd have to apply in person with my ANGLO invitation. When I opened the French windows that served as the consulate's rather grand doorway, I was surprised to discover that at least twenty people were already sitting inside, and had obviously been waiting for some time. Some were Cubans, judging from their physical appearance and clothes. Others were Swiss, waiting with their Cuban partners to get a birth certificate or have a Cuban passport renewed. And one or two were people like me, who had come to this rather un-socialist villa to apply for a visa to travel to Cuba independently.

I observed my surroundings carefully, as, in a sense, this was my first experience of Cuban culture. The villa living room was adorned with poster-sized pictures of the two Castro brothers: Fidel, the former president, and Raul, his younger brother and recent replacement. At a desk in a far, dark corner sat an elderly gentleman – the Cuban consular secretary – who could field questions in German, French, Italian, English and Spanish. He gave me a form to fill in, which then joined my passport, e-mail invitation and money in a pile of similar applications for the consul's attention. Like the Wizard of Oz, the consul existed behind a closed door, and could well have been the secretary himself, wearing another hat. I was seriously worried that my invitation would be questioned and that all my well-laid plans would fall apart at this point, so I found a seat and crossed my fingers.

The consulate was furnished in aging IKEA: three lumpy couches and about five chairs and footstools, all of them in revolutionary red. Unfortunately, they never quite managed to accommodate all the people waiting for consular attention. Part of the crowding was due to the children the Cubans had thoughtfully brought along with them. Since the children had nothing else to occupy them, the little bundles of energy were performing the useful job of testing the furniture by bouncing on and off it.

The noise in the room was probably the most disturbing factor. Cubans seem to have louder voices than Swiss or Canadians anyway, but when things got going in that living room, the volume became close to unbearable. There were, first of all, Cubans talking to other Cubans about Cuban regulations, Swiss regulations, passport, marriage and divorce regulations. There were their children, screaming and racing around the room between couch bounces. There were cell phones ringing and being answered. There was the consular secretary shushing the waiting applicants, and reminding them to take their phone conversations outdoors. All to no avail. The room resembled a classroom gone wild under a frazzled substitute teacher.

The noise came to an abrupt halt however when the consul's door opened and a dapper young man in a blazer, chinos and tasseled loafers emerged. It was the consul in person. Names were called out, passports and documents handed back by the handsome consul himself. I gratefully received my tourist card, no questions asked.

With my visa secured, I booked a plane ticket to arrive in Havana on December 8th, 2008. The flight was so far and so expensive that I decided to stay two weeks instead of one, even though I had no idea what I'd be doing besides presenting my paper at the conference and seeing Havana with Julian during the first week. I bought several guidebooks and thought I'd travel around Cuba by bus for the second week, seeing a bit of the country on my own. I was looking forward to making new Cuban friends at the conference, and, in moments of extreme optimism, I pictured myself being invited to their homes to experience the real lives of real Cubans.

I also prepared for the trip by taking a one-semester Spanish course at the university where I worked, reckoning it would at least prepare me to find a hotel or restaurant and read signs. For some reason, although I can speak German and French quite well, the Spanish language remains elusive.

The day before my flight I started thinking about what to take: summer clothes, of course – even in December – and presents. Lots of books and magazines for Julian, some vitamins for his family, soap and ballpoint pens. Maybe chocolate from Switzerland? I bought a box of fifty Swiss chocolate bars, imagining I could perhaps bribe the teachers attending my talk to say they liked it. Midway across the Atlantic, I had the brilliant idea of calling the chocolate a present to Cuban teachers from Swiss teachers. I would offer them in the name of peace and friendship.

My dream of seeing the real Cuba and understanding its people better was sometimes clouded by darker fears of Julian morphing into a Latin lover with entirely different expectations about the object of my visit. Would he prove to be a salsa-dancing gigolo? Would he want to take me out every evening to nightclubs filled with loud music and cigar-smoke? The next half hour would provide the answer.

2
ARRIVAL IN HAVANA

WE WERE DESCENDING RAPIDLY TOWARD a darkened island that looked as if it had been draped in black-out curtains. As we dropped low for the final approach, I could make out the silhouettes of palm trees and, finally, the faint lights of the airport.

Terminal 3 of José Marti International Airport was seriously underwhelming in its extent and splendor. The lighting was, once again, dim, and made me feel as if I had suddenly developed cataracts in both eyes. I was slowly getting the idea that there was some kind of restriction on electricity in Cuba. I had not realized how brightly lit our streets and public buildings are in Europe and North America. Hundreds if not thousands of the brightest light bulbs, frivolously burning away the darkness, turning it to day. Cuba's lighting made me more aware that what we call normal lighting may actually be light pollution – but since my eyes were used to western standards, airport interiors constantly appeared as if viewed through a grey film.

There wasn't much time to reflect on illumination

levels, though. I was walking towards Immigration, where I would be required to show the visa document I'd received in Bern. All passengers were lined up in front of what looked like flimsy blue outhouse doors. These led to private cubicles in which an immigration officer sat behind a high counter. My officer was a very young woman dressed in a military uniform complete with epaulettes; she almost certainly had been ordered not to smile.

"*Buenas tardes*," I beamed nervously in my recently refurbished Spanish. Frowning, she stared at my visa and passport in silence before motioning me to step back. The reason for this – which she did not explain, but which I assumed – was so that I could be photographed by an overhead camera.

"Take off espectacles," she commanded.

"Please," I added encouragingly, as I removed my glasses. I couldn't help it – the word just slipped out automatically. I held my breath, expecting to be arrested or at the very least reprimanded for talking back to an officer. Luckily, however, she seemed to interpret my "please" as an expression of compliance.

"Why you are coming to Cuba?" she asked without looking up.

"A conference – for English teachers."

"You are English teacher?"

"Yes, I am English teacher," I heard myself saying, and then heard her stamping my tourist card. I was free to enter Cuba.

Now for my suitcase, I thought. As I followed other passengers out of Immigration and into the baggage hall, I remembered the curious notice on the airport website:

There are no lockers at the airport, but
the lost and found will be of much help.

It occurred to me that this might have been an
indirect way of warning tourists that luggage was often
stolen upon arrival. I grimly approached the baggage
conveyor, where passengers from my flight were still
hoisting their bulky items over the rim: monstrous
stuffed animals, cardboard boxes full of presents, duffle
bags. Alas, my black cloth suitcase with its rainbow belt
was not among the dwindling assortment of unclaimed
objects. Rising panic threatened to overwhelm me as I
reviewed scenarios with undesirable outcomes. Then I
spotted my bag making forlorn rounds on a different belt
altogether. How it had gotten there I didn't want to know.
Joining the stream of recently arrived passengers,
I dragged my suitcase toward the exit door. Most
passengers seemed to be expatriate Cubans and their
families returning home from European exile; others
were students travelling in small groups, individual
tourists like myself and a few beach enthusiasts, in shorts
and straw hats, who had opted not to take a package trip.
A customs booth with several uniformed men loomed
ahead. Would they want to inspect the bulging suitcase
I was now trying to pull with two fingers, as if it only
contained a couple of towels instead of the many books,
pens, sunglasses, CDs and complete sets of teachers'
magazines I had brought for Julian? The nightmare I'd
had just before landing began to gnaw at the edges of my
courage. Surely the customs men would stop the family

in front of me, who were carrying obvious presents in the form of a child's hot-pink tricycle and plastic bags with many duty-free purchases. But, no, they let them pass without batting an eye – weren't even slightly interested. I was next; I looked past their heads, smiling, and they waved me through, too.

Julian and I had sent each other photos as preparation for our meeting. Nevertheless I was nervous either that something might happen and he wouldn't be there, or that he would be there but we wouldn't recognize each other. I was just reviewing the no-show plan I'd worked out, which called for me to wait one hour in the Arrivals area before phoning a hotel and taking a taxi into Havana alone, when I heard "Heather! Heather!" from the small crowd of onlookers outside the Arrivals door. Julian looked exactly like the picture he'd sent: a tall, grey-haired, bespectacled gentleman in a tweed jacket – the only person wearing one that balmy evening. He was the image of a university professor, and even had a briefcase in his hand. His voice was deep and ringing and he spoke clearly and deliberately. He seemed very sure of his English, despite what he'd written in a 2007 letter:

> I've been studying English for over 50 years, but as a non-native, I'm never quite sure of what I say or write. So please forgive any blunders I might make.

In the course of our two-year correspondence I had learned that Julian's English was very good indeed, but I'd never heard him speak before. Now at last I had the opportunity to listen to the slow and steady cadence of his sentences.

"Well, and how was your flight?" He obviously had some first questions prepared.

"It was fine – a little long, but I had a window seat and could sleep for a few hours."

"I think it is very late now in Switzerland. Are you tired?"

"Um, yeah. Let's see – well it's after 2 a.m. for me, but I don't feel that tired." I was riding an adrenaline high and feeling ecstatic that I wouldn't have to use Plan B.

"Would you like to sit down and drink something?"

"No, that's OK, I'm fine. We had a snack on the plane just before we landed."

"Well, then," inquired Julian delicately, "can we take a taxi to Havana right away?"

This reminded me of my financial responsibilities. I would of course be paying all the expenses – taxis, meals, accommodation, extras. We hadn't discussed it, but it was obvious that Julian couldn't afford to pay for anything on a salary of $24 a month.

"Sure," I said, "but first I have to get some Cuban money. There's probably an exchange around here somewhere."

And sure enough, there in the corner was a small counter announcing that it was a *cambio de divisas*. Strangely, there was only one person ahead of me at the *cambio*, also a tourist. Where was everyone else getting their Cuban money? I couldn't pursue this line of thought, however; I had just seconds to mentally calculate how much money I'd need to change for the next three to five days. I came up with 300 euros, based on nothing at all.

I'd read about the two kinds of Cuban money in the guidebooks, and Julian had also had a go at explaining the system to me in one of his letters. Basically, Cubans are paid in *pesos cubanos*, which are valid currency for all the subsidized goods and services available to Cubans; but as far as the rest of the world is concerned, the official currency is *convertibles* or CUCs, which are roughly equivalent to one US dollar. In fact, they are sometimes called *dollares*. Tourists have to pay for everything in CUCs.

"*Si?*" said the girl at the exchange counter in a bored tone of voice.

"I'd like to change euros?" I said.

"Howmuchyouwannachange?" she shot out, without raising her gaze.

"Three hundred," I answered.

This precipitated some quick manipulations with an electronic calculator. She showed me the results.

"Is good?" she said without smiling, showing me the anemic screen of her ancient calculator, while scrabbling with her other hand to get her CUCs out of a drawer.

I discreetly extracted three freshly minted 100-euro notes from a zippered belt around my waist, trying to keep my cash wad invisible. Julian was covering my back at a respectable distance. The girl counted out the CUCs in mixed denominations and noted personal details from my passport. We were done. No thank-yous.

"Well," said Julian, looking relieved that I had successfully navigated that encounter, "now we can look for the taxis. I think they are outside on the right." And indeed there were several shabby cabs lined up out there, waiting for fares. They were more of the run-down Russian Lada type than the vintage American models shown in guidebooks. After my suitcase was safely stowed in the trunk, we took off along the dark roads I'd observed from the air.

Julian was visibly relieved to sink into the back seat.

"Were you waiting a long time?" I inquired.

"Well, about three hours."

"Three hours! Why did you come out so early?"

"Well, I took the public bus from Havana and I didn't know how long it would take. You know, sometimes there are traffic ehm… traffic jams and they can be delayed."

"Oh, poor you. You must be exhausted." I had forgotten that a taxi to the airport would cost him a month's salary.

"No, it's all right. I'm just very happy you were on the plane."

"And I'm very happy you were there waiting at the airport. I wasn't too sure what I'd do if you weren't there waiting for me. I don't know Felix's last name or his address or anything."

"Oh, yes, I must tell you about Felix – there's ehm there's a little problem with your room."

Before coming out to the airport to meet me, Julian had spent the afternoon with Felix, an old friend of his who lives in a comfortable part of Havana called Vedado. When he knew for sure that I was coming to Cuba, Julian had made arrangements with Felix for me to stay as a paying guest in his apartment, which was registered as a *casa particular*, i.e. a small bed and breakfast business that Cuban citizens are allowed to run in their homes. Upon arriving at Felix's place that afternoon to make sure everything was ready, Julian heard the inconvenient news that Felix had "forgotten" to get his *casa particular* permit renewed and was therefore not legally allowed to host me as a paying guest. However all was not lost, said Felix, because he knew of a woman, his wife's second cousin in fact, who had a big apartment nearby and who also took in paying guests. My heart sank at this revelation. I had been looking forward to staying with someone Julian knew and to staying at a friendly place where Julian and I could meet to sit and talk. Besides, Felix was a professor of philosophy and I had pictured him telling me interesting, insightful things about Cuba and the Castros. But of course all I said was: "Oh, I can't stay at Felix's place? OK, OK."

3
MEETING MAGDALENA

"**F**IRST WE WILL GO TO your *casa particular* and leave your luggage; then we can go out for a drink – if you are willing," Julian suggested, as we seemed to be approaching the end of the taxi ride from the airport. "Your landlady – can I say landlady? – her name is Magdalena. I only met her this afternoon, when Felix took me to meet her. Her location is excellent, really excellent. You will see."

I could barely make out the shapes of buildings on Magdalena's street. It was only a little past 9 p.m. and I couldn't believe all the things that had transpired in the last fourteen hours. I'd flown from Zurich to Paris to Cuba, I'd breezed through immigration with my visa from Bern and then walked through customs, dragging a suitcase full of books and other presents with no trouble whatsoever. It suddenly seemed miraculous that I was sitting in a taxi with the man I'd been exchanging letters with for the past two years.

Now the street brightened considerably on the left, as our taxi stopped across from the palm-lined driveway of that famous Havana landmark, the Hotel Nacional. I quickly extracted some Cuban money from my purse and slipped it to Julian, saying: "This is for any expenses." He took it discreetly with a smile and a nod.

The driver paid, we dragged my suitcase up the shadowy front steps of a smart-looking apartment house, through heavy wrought-iron gating and across a once-elegant marble lobby to a dirty piece of unpainted plywood placed where an elevator would normally be. I pulled the plywood by its makeshift handle; it *was* an elevator, but it lacked lighting. Feeling our way, we maneuvered the suitcase into the dark and dangling contraption and pushed the top button for the tenth floor. Distant clanking and the hum of moving cable; we started to rise. I looked upward through the cable-hole in the roof of the lift and glimpsed the starry sky twinkling above the shaft of this Otis elevator that must have been in service for what... over 50 years? Did I detect sounds of fraying cable?

We emerged via another makeshift door on the tenth floor. A quiet, white marble corridor with each of its four doors guarded by a small wrought-iron gate. Julian pushed the second doorbell, which buzzed loudly, and soon we heard the voice of a woman repeatedly screeching "Julian?" as she approached the door. After reassurances from Julian, she undid three locks.

Julian introduced me to Magdalena in Spanish as we entered. She was in her mid-seventies, a little over five feet tall and stocky, with warm brown eyes and short, frizzy hair tinted reddish-brown. Her face was full and pleasant; her housecoat, faded and pink. As she led us through the narrow kitchen to the living room, it became apparent that her vision was in some way impaired: she always stared to the right or left of what she wanted to see. She moved around her apartment easily, however, recognizing every counter edge and doorknob by touch. And she never once stopped talking. I was relieved to have Julian with me to help with the Spanish.

"Well, what she is telling," he murmured in a low voice as Magdalena rattled on, "is that the elevator sometimes breaks down and that the apartment house committee – you know we have local committees to manage things like that – the committee is, ehm,… lazy about repairs. And she says she can't walk down the stairway from the tenth floor due to her poor eyesight."

Then he said to Magdalena: "*No, no, claro que no.*"

Magdalena had meanwhile extended the elevator rant to include the whole country, complaining – as far as I could follow – about shortages and stupid decisions. I mentally noted that here at least was one Cuban who was not afraid to protest – loudly and to strangers – about life under the Castro brothers.

We followed Magdalena into her large living room and sat down on the green velvet chairs, which were all turned towards the ancient television occupying a shelf on the far wall. The fact that we were all facing in the same direction made conversation somewhat strange, but this did not concern Magdalena as she had something urgent on her mind. The problem was that, like Felix, she hadn't bothered to renew her *casa particular* permit with the police, and now that I'd actually materialized, she was starting to get cold feet. She had already phoned her daughter about it, who'd said not to worry, the police would never know, but Magdalena wasn't so sure: the

27

neighbors would notice. Some of them, especially the zealous pro-Castro woman on the ground floor, who seemed to be a sort of caretaker-cum-block captain, would certainly report her if she got wind of my presence.

"*No, no, senora,*" I heard Julian reassuring her in Spanish, "Heather will not be here so much and they'll never notice her. And if they do,... if they ask, she could be your relative from Canada. It's possible, no?"

"*Ah si,*" Magdalena agreed. "*Es possible – ella podria ser mi prima por ejemplo.*" I could be her cousin who was just visiting and not paying anything. So I was to learn my Spanish sentence about being Magdalena's Canadian cousin and, if anyone asked, everything would appear to be fine and above-board. That lifted the clouds of worry for the present. We could now go and see where I was going to sleep.

My bedroom had its own private bathroom and was located on the far side of the kitchen from Magdalena's living quarters. It was comfortably furnished and by no means the spartan cell I had envisioned. The wall at the head of my bed was covered floor-to-ceiling with flowered cloth curtains. Opposite this were four shuttered, glassless windows looking out over rooftops towards the sea. The salty smell of the warm Atlantic was a faint presence in the room.

Magdalena gave me an elaborate tour of the sparse furniture, showing me where I could put my things: a chest of drawers, each drawer freshly lined with newspaper, a chair in front of the window, hooks on the back of the door, drawers in the night table, and a closet with four badly mangled wire hangers. Further amenities were a

Spanish guidebook for Havana that was only twenty years old and a night table with a fascinating three-way lamp that lit up when one touched its base. Then, a pink-tiled bathroom off the bedroom with a normal-looking toilet, sink and tub. Perfect. The tour-de-room was drawing to a close.

"Are you still willing to go across to the Hotel Nacional and have a drink?" Julian asked with a kindly twinkle. I felt wide-awake and ready to go, even though it was by now 10 p.m. – or 4 a.m., Zurich time.

"Will it still be open so late at night?" I wondered.

"Well, it's a hotel! It must be open."

So I shoved my suitcase into the closet, picked up my handbag and we were off to the rickety elevator again – and to the balmy Havana night.

As we strolled across the street towards the open doors of the bright hotel lobby, I began to take in the vintage Oldsmobile and Cadillac convertibles parked in its driveway. Faint music wafted out on a sea-humid breeze, and we entered the glamorous setting of a forties movie: uniformed bellboys and doormen, a kiosk devoted to cigars, signs pointing to ballrooms and elegant dining rooms, lots of marble and mahogany. Standing around in the lobby were clusters of artsy-looking people, some wearing sunglasses at ten in the evening. Julian steered me to a cozy little room with a bar in it and dozens of photographs on the walls, most of them signed. They commemorated famous guests of yesteryear, like Winston Churchill, Nat King Cole, Frank Sinatra, Ernest Hemingway, Ava Gardner, Pablo Casals, Mickey

Mantle… And here we were, just the two of us, alone with all this history.

A thin line of jazz trickled down a keyboard in the background. I felt like Lauren Bacall.

"Do you like *mojitos*?" Julian inquired.

"I've never had one actually. They're made with rum, aren't they?"

"Yes, rum and *menta* – that's mint – and tonic and ice. Would you like to try one?"

"Umm, yes, I *would* like to try one… very much… but maybe not tonight. The rum might give me a headache. I guess I'd better have something else this evening."

"Yes, you have had a long day, of course. Maybe a cola or juice?"

I didn't want to be a wet blanket, but I knew that alcohol after the day's stress would almost certainly result in waking up with a pounder. So much for Lauren Bacall.

We sat there with our drinks, talking as if we'd known each other for much longer than two hours, which we had, of course: I already knew quite a bit about Julian's family and his work. That he lived in Santa Clara, a city in central Cuba, that he taught classes in medical English at the medical university and had been active – instrumental even – in developing a new curriculum of medical English for all medical students in his province. That he loved reading, especially books about cognitive psychology, modern history, and his hero, the Cuban writer and liberator, José Marti.

And he knew the same sorts of things about me: that I was a sixty-three-year-old single Canadian woman, schooled in the United States but now living and working in Switzerland, where I taught English for scientific purposes at the University of Zurich. That I, too, was interested in cognitive psychology, but, unlike him, also loved reading novels and listening to classical music. That I spent a lot of my free time outdoors, hiking or cycling with my companion, Helga. And that the rest of my family lived in Canada and the US.

"Well and how are your parents?" inquired Julian.

"They're doing pretty well, considering their ages: my dad's going to be ninety next year and he's still working on an article he wants to submit to a medical journal."

"Heh heh. That's really wonderful for such an age. Do you think he will finish it?"

"Not sure – maybe. He says he wants to send it to me for editing when I get back to Switzerland."

On the opposite wall I noticed a large plaque commemorating what I translated to myself as "the club of over-a-hundred".

"Yes," said Julian, "there are many Cubans who live to be over the age of one hundred. Can you see the ages on that list? 116, 110, 105…"

"Wow, that's incredible. Why are there so many people here who live so long?"

"Well, of course it could be their genes, but it's also because of diet, I think. In ehm in what we call the "special period in a time of peace" – you know, in the 1990s, when the Soviet Union collapsed and stopped supporting Cuba economically – most Cubans didn't really have enough to eat. Not enough calories. It was a very, very hard time. So you didn't see any fat people, almost none. And I think this could also be the ehm the reason why there are so many Cubans who reach an age of over one hundred years."

———————— ••• ————————

By eleven o'clock, despite the magical ambience of the hotel, despite my elation at having arrived safely in Cuba, despite the thrill of finally talking to Julian in person, my eyes were falling shut.

"I think I should take you back to Magdalena's," Julian said with a grin. He settled the bill at the bar with our spending money and we wandered back down the long, elegant driveway to the darkened gates of Magdalena's apartment house. The stars had come closer; the sea-air caressed. Julian made sure I could let myself into the lobby with Magdalena's key and then, making a small bow, disappeared into the darkness of Havana.

As we'd done two hours previously, I crossed the lobby, opened the plywood door and entered the ancient Otis elevator, feeling for the tenth-floor button in the dark. The cabin jerked upwards, rose to a height of perhaps five feet and then stopped. I waited for a full minute to see if anyone had pressed a button somewhere else and thereby halted the lift. Absolute silence. Oh no, I thought. I'm stuck between floors in this death-crate; it's late, nobody will hear me if I shout, and what should I shout in Spanish anyway? What's the Spanish word for help? They don't teach you useful words like that in a Spanish course. I pressed another button. Nothing. Then I had the brilliant idea of pressing the bottom button. The elevator lurched again and proceeded to lower me gently to the ground floor, where I was more than happy to make my exit.

There was only one solution as far as I was concerned: the narrow stairway next to the lift. With a singing heart I took the stairs to the tenth floor two at a time, meeting no one, checking floor numbers as I went, fairly out of breath, but safe and happy. And, just to stay on the safe side, I used the stairway instead of the elevator every day thereafter, thus increasing my chances of joining the over-a-hundred club.

As I soundlessly let myself into my room at Magdalena's, I noted that the living room TV was no longer blaring, which meant that she had probably gone to bed. After all, it was quite late, even for Havana – or *La Habana*, as I was already starting to say in my head.

My gaze travelled around the room: the floral curtained wall, the pink chenille bedspread on the double bed, the humble, well-worn chair and dresser and three-tap lamp on the night table, the familiar American porcelain fittings in the bathroom. That was the thing: this room – my own little room in Cuba – did not feel very foreign at all. But in other ways Cuba felt very different: being dependent on Julian for communication, being careful not to talk politics in public, the darkness that cloaked everything outside in the streets, the many coffee-colored people I'd noticed working in the hotel. Another difference was that there was no glass at all in my bedroom window, and even though it was the eighth of December, balmy ocean air was wafting through the wooden shutters. I fell asleep lulled by the waves of the Atlantic hitting the seawall beyond the Nacional, smiling at my good luck in knowing Julian and being in Cuba.

4
FIRST IMPRESSIONS

As I EMERGED FROM A sound sleep, the warm Atlantic breeze was still drifting into my bedroom, reminding me that I was far from Zurich. The distant sound of waves slapping a wall drew me from my bed to peer out through the dark green slats. It was just after six, and the sun was already shining from behind our building onto the dimpling waves of a slightly choppy sea. One or two small boats – no doubt fishermen and not escapees – moved soundlessly toward the horizon. There was virtually no motor traffic to disturb the serenity.

A couple of blocks to the left, a vast, curved apartment house dominated the skyline, its windows reflecting the progress of the rising sun. I wondered who had built it – Batista? Castro? – and who lived there now. It looked futuristic in an old-fashioned way, like Gotham in a Superman comic, and made me think of Stalin's over-dimensioned apartment houses in Moscow.

Just then, an insistent gurgling started up in all the pipes of our apartment: somewhere, a lot of water had been turned on. The previous evening, Magdalena had placed a bucket of warm water in my bathroom while I was out with Julian; this, I assumed, was because there was no warm water tap. But now my ears told me that water for my bathroom was running into a large tank above the bathtub. By following the pipes I realized that this same tank was emptied every time I flushed the toilet or turned on the tap; there was no running water direct from the mains.

I opened my bedroom door to find Magdalena in her faded pink housecoat, filling buckets and basins from various taps in the kitchen.

"*Hay agua,*" she commented over her shoulder. "There's water."

"*Si, si, hay agua,*" I agreed sagely. Then, after waiting and watching for a minute so as not to appear too pushy, I made my request:

"*Perdon. Es possible tomar una ducha*?" hoping that it meant, more or less, "Excuse me, could I possibly have a shower?"

"*Como no,*" was the answer. "Of course."

She immediately shut off her taps to come into my bathroom and show me how the shower worked. I was grateful for this because I'd been wondering how to deal with the complex metal contraption over my bathtub, which resembled nothing so much as a tin percolator basket connected to taps and a wire. Magdalena reached up, turned a tiny tap and pushed a button, showing me how this lit a small gas flame that heated water running through a narrow pipe. This very hot water was then mixed with water from another pipe until it was the right temperature. So all I had to do – while standing there naked – was turn a tap and simultaneously produce a gas flame by means of a minor explosion.

Now, as I'm the sort of person who feels nervous in the mere presence of propane tanks and balloons, this arrangement was less than comforting. The thought that I might not shower for two weeks briefly flitted through my mind. But no, I told myself, I'm here partly out of solidarity, to find out what it's like to live in a run-down socialist country, where nothing works and everything is rationed; I have to try a shower with this percolator-thing or die trying. So I undressed in preparation for my first Cuban shower, turned on the gas and pushed the spark button. The gas lit with a sharp little pop, and as I turned the tap for more water, the flame responded with more heat. This might just work, I decided, frowning warily at the tamed contraption.

Having survived trial-by-shower, I emerged from my bedroom, dressed and glowing, ready for breakfast and my first day in Havana. Magdalena had finished collecting water from the kitchen taps and had started heating a large cauldron of water on the gas stove. This, she explained, was to produce safe drinking water, which she showed me how to get for myself from the fridge. Julian had warned me not to drink any tap water the night before, so I was glad Magdalena provided such a copious supply. As I looked down the long, narrow kitchen, I noted two fridges – a pre-revolutionary dwarf and a new white giant – between which stood a large enamel sink and its draining board. Across from the sink there was an old gas stove and lots of counter space with built-in cupboards above and below. A low, round table at the far end completed the furnishings. There were glassless windows over the stove too, with the same open-slatted shutters as in my bedroom.

"*Todo bien?*" inquired Magdalena.

"*Si, si*," I responded, "*muy bien.*"

"*Quiere un café?*"

"*No, gracias. Prefiero tee.*" I smiled and dangled one of the tea bags I'd brought with me.

"*Ah, no toma café? Quiere yogul, o pan, o guayaba?*"

Yogul sounded a lot like yogurt, *pan* I knew was bread and *guayaba* was guava, a fruit that Julian had brought from Santa Clara as a present. I said, "*Si, por favor*" and then added "*Gracias*", just in case that wasn't polite enough. The yogurt turned out to be made from soybeans and was quite good, but the fresh guava was a revelation: its pungent, sweet flavor and vivid pink flesh won me over immediately. I wanted to eat one of those every day.

As we sat at the kitchen table having our breakfast, Magdalena was determined to make conversation, despite my backwardness in Spanish. She started with the basics: my family and where I lived. I dashed off to get my pocket dictionary from my handbag and returned to the table fingering it nervously.

"*Usted vive en Suiza, no?*" she got down to business.

"*Si a Zurich.*"

"*Y su familia? Donde viven?*"

"*Mi familia?*" I told her that my parents and siblings were spread around Canada and the US, but that I lived in Switzerland.

"*Sola? No esta casada?*" Her eyebrows shot up.

No, I told her, I wasn't married.

And so the interrogation ran on. If I wasn't married, she wanted to know, what did I do for a living, what did my parents do, how did I know Julian, and so on. After a while, when she'd figured out that I could understand about ten times as much as I could say, she told me things far more interesting to us both: about her own family, about her beautiful and intelligent grandchildren, about one daughter who'd married into the Castro family but then divorced, and about another who'd studied chemistry and physics but now worked in a tourist shop, where she made good money.

Julian rescued me at 8.30, when he picked me up for our first day of sightseeing. No longer wearing the tweed jacket of the previous evening, he had switched to a polo-shirt and a baseball cap; in fact he looked a lot like a tourist himself. He'd had a good night's sleep in the dormitory of the Havana dental school, where he'd booked a bed at reasonable cost and was only a fifteen-minute walk from Magdalena's. Julian and Magdalena exchanged morning pleasantries, but he refused to sit down for a cup of coffee.

"I've been finding out about Esther." Magdalena reported with pride. For her, my name was – and always would be – Esther. "Her father is nearly ninety, you know?"

"Yes, I know," Julian answered, "he's a medical professor and he's writing an article."

"*Si*. About the heart and blood. Heart attacks are terrible, *terrible*. My cousin in Las Tunas had a heart attack last month, you know. A heart attack – standing in a pharmacy, yes he was. He'd gone there because he had a pain – a bad pain in his left arm, you know? And then…"

"Hmm, yes, well I think we really ought to…"

"… luckily the pharmacist recognized the symptoms and called the ambulance. Luis lives alone – his wife left him years ago, *years* ago – so it was much, much better to be in hospital than to die alone at home. But then he…"

"*Senora*, I'm extremely sorry for your cousin," interrupted Julian, "but we have to leave. Heather's never going to see Havana if we don't get started now."

The morning was sunny and pleasant, so we decided to walk from Vedado, the relatively genteel district of Havana where Magdalena lived, to Habana Vieja, the old town and starting point of most tourist activities. I'd often told Julian how much I enjoyed hiking in the mountains of Switzerland and so he'd obliged me by planning a long walk.

As we stepped out of Magdalena's apartment house on Calle O and proceeded downhill toward the street known as La Rampa, I was immediately aware that Havana sidewalks require more attention than Swiss ones. In fact, they are a veritable minefield of deep holes, major items of garbage, dog dirt and – worst of all – the jagged remains of street signs that have been sawn off about six inches above the ground. I couldn't believe it. Who could be so indifferent to public safety as to saw off metal signposts with six rusty inches still sticking out of the concrete?

We turned left onto La Rampa, heading for the sea wall, passing neatly dressed men and women standing in queues, waiting for buses, presumably to go to work. We then followed the Malecon towards the center of the city, walking along the shady building-side of the wide avenue, not the sunny sea-side. My corner-of-the-eye exploration of the Havanese environment continued as Julian described Havana's geography and explained features of Cuban life.

"That tall building is a well-known hospital, named Los Hermanos Ameijeiras, the brothers Ameijeiras. It is a teaching hospital and very well known. Foreigners from all over the world come here for operations. A former student of mine is now one of the head surgeons there."

"Oh that reminds me," I said. "I saw a huge building out my bedroom window this morning. Sort of curved? It looks like a big apartment house and is near the Malecon – about two blocks from Magdalena's place."

"Oh yes, I ehm I presume you are describing the FOCSA building. It's the tallest building in Cuba. Once it was very fashionable for Cubans to live there in Batista's time. I think it is being repaired now."

We walked on resolutely. Small short-haired dogs of no particular race lay on the sidewalk, basking in the morning rays, sleeping away the hours till their next meal. Salsa music pulsed from several dingy bars that seemed to be recovering from a hard night's use. The sparse traffic (consisting of American cars from the fifties and sixties, a few buses and funny scooter-taxis with giant yellow bowling-ball backs) was increasing.

"What kind of vehicle is that?"

"Ah. Those are called coco-taxis because they look like... ehm I think you say coconuts?"

"It looks like it might be fun to ride in one."

"Mhm, yes. Then we can take one some time, if you are willing."

We were walking at a fairly brisk pace past the buildings and narrow streets of Havana Centro, the less photogenic district of Havana that lies between Vedado and the old town. Julian made a point of always walking on the street-side of the sidewalk. We both racked our brains for easy topics as we adjusted to each other's expectations, interests and English.

"It's good that you have a hat," Julian commented. "The sun is stronger here than in northern countries. I must always be careful with the sun – even in winter."

"Yeah, that's true," I replied. "Do many people here get skin cancer?"

"Oh yes, yes, quite a number of Caucasians. I have to be careful to wear sunglasses, too, because ehm exposure to a lot of bright sun can lead to cataracts."

I promised myself I'd always wear sunglasses in the future.

We passed dusty, derelict four– and five-story apartment buildings with badly tilting balconies that had been fenced off and abandoned, then slightly less derelict ones with men – young and old – sitting on the front steps or on the curb just watching the traffic go by. Women were scarcer and, if visible, were mopping floors, hanging laundry on balconies or carrying bags of shopping.

After a good half-hour of steady walking, we finally turned right onto a broad boulevard with a bench-lined promenade running down the middle. The state of the apartment buildings now changed noticeably: gorgeously renovated buildings were much more common, many of them pale coral, powder blue or lime, with their arched galleries and ornate balconies restored to the elegant Spanish and Moorish styles of the early twentieth century. One building looked almost like a pink and white mosque, with curving stucco columns and exotically shaped arches.

"These buildings are absolutely gorgeous, Julian." I pulled out my camera.

"Yes, that is mostly the restoration work of the Cuban architect Eusebio Leal. He has been charged by Fidel with restoring the buildings of Old Havana to bring back its ehm previous elegance. He's also a historian and knows more than anyone about the city, so I'm very happy that you noticed his work. It is inspiring for all Cubans. Sometimes he makes programs about his projects for the television."

The broad promenade with its white marble benches and paving tiles continued, the traffic banned to narrow lanes on either side. Children in uniforms consisting of neat maroon shorts or skirts and a white shirt were making their way to school, accompanied by a parent or grandparent. Older citizens were sitting on the stone benches, reading newspapers in the clear morning sunlight or talking to a neighbor. The scene was idyllic.

"This boulevard is called Paseo de Marti or Paseo del Prado," explained Julian. "It was of course a very fashionable place to live in the past." It wasn't hard to imagine the opulent lifestyle of inhabitants in the early decades of the twentieth century; now, however, the buildings seemed to house less wealthy citizens.

Julian pointed out other places of more recent

historical interest to me, but I couldn't stop admiring the loveliness of the restorations. It was also heartening to see three– and four-story buildings in the center of a city. This is how an inner city ought to look, I thought: like a backdrop for human interaction, not like a canyon of high walls that make humans appear insignificant.

Finally, we came to what seemed like the end of the Prado. Across the street from us, near a statue of the national hero, José Marti, I could observe clusters of men gesticulating wildly as they engaged in animated discussion. Julian chuckled:

"Oh, those are the big baseball fans. They are going over and over controversial ehm actions in past Cuban baseball games. They are arguing about what should have been done or what the… do you say referee?… what he should have decided."

I was once again amazed. "About *past* baseball games? How often do they meet?" I wanted to know.

"Oh every day. Yes, yes, they meet every day on that street corner and argue about past baseball games. It's their hobby," he grinned and shook his head.

Julian and I then entered the pedestrian zone of Habana Vieja (Old Havana) and headed down Calle del Obispo or Bishop Street. The first thing I spotted was the Floridita bar, made famous by Ernest Hemingway. Taking a discreet look through the doorway, we caught sight of a life-size bronze likeness of the American writer, leaning against the bar. We passed half-empty government-owned bookshops, old-fashioned clothing shops, and salsa-blaring cafés. What struck me most about one of the best-known pedestrian shopping streets in Havana was the absence of commercial advertising. There were no large signs over the stores, no special deals announced in the store windows; just items for sale and hand-written prices. There wasn't even any graffiti. What was more, not every available inch was exploited for commercial gain: every two blocks or so there was an inviting little park with palms or other trees, lots of benches, maybe a fountain. Locals of all ages seemed to be using these parks as a living room. Elderly, down-at-heel inhabitants emerged from narrow doorways to shuffle over to an Obispo park; mothers and young children sat down in them to play and wait for older siblings to finish school.

Peering through the glassless ground-floor window of a shabby structure, I saw what looked like a classroom full of small children sitting at desks in front of their teacher. Was this a neighborhood primary school in such an old building?

"Yes, it's a school for young children," Julian answered my questioning gaze. He explained that schools in Habana Vieja were generally not in separate school buildings, but in the rooms of existing structures. The children seemed interested in their instruction and not easily distracted by passing pedestrians.

We next passed ETECSA, the state telephone company. People were lined up in the street, waiting to be admitted to the building one-by-one to pay their phone bill or make a phone call; each time a customer exited, another was let in by a guard. I had read about ETECSA in my guidebook, which said it sold internet access to foreigners. Julian thought that this might indeed be the place where tourists could buy a card for internet time; I promised myself that I would return later to email home.

"Now we are coming to a really beautiful part of Havana." Julian took my arm and guided me into a sunny plaza with a huge church at one end.

"This is Cathedral Square," he announced proudly.

A five-man *son* group was making music on the sidewalk: two guitars, bongos, a rattle and woodblock. It was all I could do not to walk in time to the music – I was feeling so happy and carefree. Julian had turned out to be just what I had expected from his letters: interesting, humorous, kind. I was having a great time discovering beautiful old Havana. The air was warm, the city was pedestrian-friendly and I felt safe. We stopped at tables set up in the square in front of El Patio restaurant and ordered two large glasses of fresh *guayaba* juice. I still couldn't believe that I had lived my whole long life without the marvelous taste of guava.

Sitting in the shade of the Patio's parasols, we observed tall creole women strolling across the plaza in elegant colonial costumes, posing for photos with tourists, to whom they also tried to sell cigars or kisses. Suddenly, a middle-aged and shabbily-dressed man appeared out of nowhere and asked me if I had a pen for him. Taken by surprise, I shook my head. "You have little soap?" he suggested. Again, I shook my head, feeling fairly uncomfortable, but also steeling myself for more intense begging. I expected Julian to parry the man's requests just as I had, but instead he took a small coin from his pocket – a coin of his own money – and, saying "*Aqui*

45

tiene" (Here you are), gave it to the man, who – staring at the paltry gift with incredulity – wandered off.

"There are many people in Cuba who have far less than I have," explained Julian. "It doesn't hurt to give them something." I felt ashamed of my selfishness, which was actually due to fear of becoming personally involved. I was afraid the man wouldn't leave us alone if I gave him something. Julian wasn't afraid of that, and his charity probably represented two or three hours' pay in terms of his salary, although in dollars it was next to nothing. Privately, I vowed I'd be less rigid with beggars in future.

The music group continued to fill the square with syncopated melody, and it wasn't long before three or four elderly bystanders, all of them locals, stood up and started dancing alone. They must have been eighty if they were a day, but they all had the cool, minimal moves of Latin dancers and swung their hips with easy elegance.

"Can you dance like that?" I asked Julian.

He laughed. "No, not at all. I am not a dancer and I have never been one."

"But what about when you were younger? Didn't you dance then – to meet girls, for instance?"

"Heh heh. I was pretty serious as a student, you know, and very shy. I listened to a lot of music on the radio, but I never imagined dancing with it. What about you?"

"Oh sure, I used to dance as a teenager, but not much since then. And I know for a fact that I'm terrible at salsa or anything with subtle movements. A couple of years ago, when I was at a conference in Turkey, a professional dancer asked me to dance salsa with him in front of about three hundred people. I was a clumsy failure and it's still one of my most embarrassing memories."

"That's fine, then. You don't expect that I will ask you to dance?"

"No! I'll be relieved if you don't," I laughed. So the dancing question was settled once and for all, and I knew that the chances of Julian turning into a Latin lover were very close to zero.

Two hours later, after lunch and a visit to a museum of colonial life, we were seated on a bench under tall trees in the Plaza de Armas at the end of Obispo. The little square also contained shelf upon shelf of second-hand books, set up as a sales display. There were dozens of books on recent Cuban history, biographies of Fidel and Che, Spanish novels, periodicals, and even a few books in English. The prices were very low by western standards. To my surprise, Julian showed great interest in some of the books displayed, even though they were twenty or thirty years old.

"I am a bibliophile," he confessed, "and I can't help loving books. They were my whole world when I was a boy, when I was alone at home with just my mother and no brothers or sisters."

"Yes. I like books a lot, too," I answered, "but these books are out of date. Surely you can get new books now with better information."

"Mhm, maybe so, but you can still learn a lot from old books – and, you know, if you read them, you are in a way keeping them alive."

It was then that I thought to myself: yes that's what seems to be happening here. Cubans have been forced by historic circumstance to give new life to outdated things. Buildings, elevators, fridges, books – even baseball games. Nothing is torn down. Nothing is discarded. Everything is repaired and recycled for further use; things go on and on and on, which makes Cuba a little like a living museum of the last sixty years. It's famous for its photogenic 1950s cars, lovingly preserved DeSotos, Chevvies and Pontiacs that are parked and driven and worked on in every neighborhood. But the same thing happens to a lot of other household goods that we'd call obsolete: they enjoy an unplanned immortality in Cuba's struggle to continue.

———

On the evening of our first day together, Julian and I were sitting outdoors in the garden of the Hotel Nacional across the street from Magdalena's. We were recovering from the day's sightseeing by drinking *mojitos*, which the bartender assured me were highly refreshing and not so terribly full of rum. The air was no longer hot, and as we gazed at the ocean from our deep-cushioned couch, the tall palms in the garden rustled in the onshore breeze.

"So, Heather," began Julian, smiling expectantly, "what do you think of Cuba after your first day here?"

"I like it very, very much," I answered truthfully, "It's partly what I expected – people have far fewer material possessions than where I live. But here people seem to appreciate the basics much more, too. I don't know – could it be that the economic situation allows them to recognize the essence, the core of things more clearly?"

"Yes, it's interesting that you noticed that. I didn't see it so clearly before, but what you say is true. And your appreciation of – as you say – of the essential core of things is probably why you like Cuba."

5

MIRACLES AND
CIVIL SOCIETY

WHILE I WAS PLANNING MY trip to Cuba, a Zurich neighbor had shown me his black-and-white photographs of a vast Havana cemetery, overflowing with lugubrious sensuality. All the monuments were of white marble: elaborate statues of mourning humans and angels, loyal dogs, the holy family, famous residents and heroes. I wanted to see it and take my own artsy pictures, so I told Julian that the Necropolis de Colon was one of the places in Havana that I absolutely had to visit.

Since the cemetery was in the same district as Magdalena's apartment, I'd suggested walking there, just as we'd walked into Habana Vieja on our first day of sightseeing. However it turned out to be more tiring and less pleasant than anticipated, because we had to walk the scorching length of Calle 21 for over a mile. The neighborhood was mostly residential at first, but then changed into a treeless zone, lined with workshops and businesses. Julian was wearing a black shirt and carrying his heavy briefcase with our water bottles in it, and I was also in unnecessarily warm clothes. Together we trudged the endless blocks to the Cemetery of Christopher Columbus, which is the cemetery's name in English.

The cemetery certainly lived up to its reputation as the largest in Latin America. Tombs and mausoleums of all styles and proportions lined the broad lanes within it – an immense, crowded metropolis of grieving statuary. As we strolled through, Julian pointed out the tombs of famous Cuban writers and politicians, most of whom I had never heard of. But it was not only for the famous. I can remember a tower-like monument dedicated to scores of firemen who had died fighting a major fire in 1890, each hero's individual likeness captured in the relief around the base.

After walking past legions of weeping angels and moping cherubs, we came to possibly the most famous and tragic grave of all: it is called *la Milagrosa*, the miraculous one. The story Julian told me runs as follows. Early in the 20th century, Amelia, the wife of a well-to-do businessman, died in childbirth. Because her death was closely followed by that of her infant son, they were placed in the same coffin and entombed in the Necropolis de Colon, where her grieving husband came to visit their sarcophagus every day. His belief was that Amelia was not dead, but only asleep, and so he developed the habit of knocking on her tomb, calling "Wake up, Amelia". Later on, when for some reason the coffin was re-opened, Amelia's body was discovered to be uncorrupted by decay, which, according to Catholic belief, is a sure sign of sainthood. The most extraordinary discovery, however, was that her child, who had been laid at her feet in the coffin, was now in her arms. A statue of Amelia embracing a cross with one arm and her son with the other was erected at the head of the sarcophagus. Today, people who feel affected by the story, particularly if they have lost or are afraid of losing a child, still come to the gravesite and pray to Amelia, always making sure that they never turn their back on the statue. Julian told me this story while we stood to one side, watching a steady queue of women, one after the other, pray before Amelia's statue and then leave a small bouquet on the tomb as they backed away from the statue's gaze.

"So, Heather," he murmured as we moved on, "what do you think is the explanation for this miracle?"

Being skeptical by nature, I had already thought of one. "Hmm. Well the part about the baby being in her arms – could it be that the coffin was shaken up a little when it was transported? Or, maybe, that the baby was actually placed in her arms before burial?"

"Yes. That is a real possibility… But what about her body? There was no decay."

"Right. That's harder to explain. Do you have a theory?"

"Well, I am not an expert, but I can imagine that the ehm coffin was sealed so tightly, you know, it may have been airless – can I say airless?"

"Airtight."

"Thank you, airtight,… and then such a phenomenon might be possible. Or it could be a miracle, of course," he added with a grin.

"We all believe in some miracles, I guess."

"Indeed, indeed. You know, there's a Cuban medical program called Operation Miracle that brings surgical eye care to poor regions in other Latin American countries. Also, many people from Latin America are flown to Cuba for free for treatment by our doctors. That's a more practical kind of miracle – and a very big one too."

———————••———————

After less than an hour of trying and failing to take the aesthetically stunning photos I'd hoped for, I gave up. It was too sunny, and everything looked flat and far too colorful and cluttered. Besides, it was getting extremely hot. It was time to go back the way we'd come. As we waited to cross a busy and shadeless intersection, Julian announced that he wanted to invite me to lunch. This was because he had vowed that he would pay for us whenever prices were in Cuban pesos, and he'd noticed more than one government-subsidized peso-restaurant on our way to the cemetery. So as we continued homeward, wilted and hungry, Julian stopped a man who looked like a local and asked, "*Companero*, tell me, is there a good peso restaurant near here?"

"*Si si. Un bueno*," was the reply, "in the next block, on the corner."

Peso-restaurants serve a three-course meal for something like twenty cents. Tourists are discouraged – if not actually barred – from eating at these highly subsidized places, and so a major problem for me would be that I felt embarrassed to be eating subsidized food intended for people with massively lower incomes than mine. Nevertheless, I was curious to experience something that was for Cubans and not for tourists, so I accepted Julian's invitation to have lunch there. The interior was cool, high-ceilinged and blandly functional, with tables and chairs from the 1950s. The menu revealed a limited choice of three items for each course; Julian and I ordered roast chicken and vegetables, preceded by soup and followed by flan – all for twenty cents.

Unfortunately, I couldn't exactly relax and enjoy the meal. We'd decided to switch to speaking Spanish in the restaurant because we didn't want to underline the fact that I was a foreign tourist, although the staff had probably noticed this from the way I looked and moved the moment I stepped in the door. Needless to say, sounding Cuban proved something of a challenge for me. Whenever the waiter was nearby, Julian did all the talking, with only the odd *si* or *por que*? from me. Our one-sided conversation went something like this:

Julian: *La sopa es muy rica. Te gusta*? (The soup is delicious. Do you like it?)

Heather: *Si, me gusta mucho.* (Yes, very much.)

Julian: *Y es muy bueno para la recuperacion de la sal despues de sudar.* (And it's very good for restoring salt after sweating.)

Heather: *Si, es muy bueno.* (Yes, it's very good.)

And so on.

The food in the subsidized restaurant lacked neither quality nor taste; however the whole atmosphere was strangely impersonal and bureaucratic. The waiters served the food without smiling or trying to please; the typewritten menu was stained and in small print; the food was plonked rather than arranged appetizingly on the plates; the gray-faced guests, all apparently office workers with a job in the neighborhood, sat alone or in pairs, eating quietly or chatting discreetly. There were no signs or colors; absolutely no commercial allure – no special deals of the day, no encouragement to drink anything other than water. So this is what a non-capitalist restaurant looks like, I thought; no incentives to consume and spend more than is absolutely necessary. It was interesting – even laudable – but hard to get used to. I realized just how much our appetites are shaped by constant exposure to commercial enticement.

Watching Julian count out his hard-earned money caused me to reflect on the true justice of his paying for everything priced in Cuban pesos, while I paid for everything charged in CUCs. For the sake of fairness, I decided to compare the hours Julian and I spent earning the money we paid. When I paid for a lunch priced in CUCs, I was paying with about twenty minutes' worth of work; but when Julian paid for our lunch in the peso restaurant, he was spending nearly three hours' worth of work. It wasn't really fair at all.

On our first day in Habana Vieja, Julian and I had had lunch in a small, privately owned restaurant called La Marina that we'd discovered by ourselves on the corner of Oficios and Teniente Rey. We chose the restaurant mainly because the menu looked tasty and reasonable: we could get a whole lunch of salad, meat or fish and vegetables with rice, dessert and a beer for six CUCs each. But we also favored it because we could eat on an outdoor patio, screened from public view by tropical plants, and without loud music. La Marina was apparently run by a family of four or five adults, who did the cooking, bar-keeping and serving, and who kept asking guests if they liked the food. The atmosphere was friendly and welcoming, and there was even a job for "Grandfather", who sat by the doors to the *servicios* and made sure only restaurant guests used the toilets.

A further attraction of La Marina was the sugarcane press in the corner. When we first sat down to lunch, it was not in use, but as the lunch hour wore on, a man appeared and started operating the simple machine. He turned a large metal hand-wheel that caused stalks of sugarcane to be drawn through a press, squeezing out their sweet juice or *guarapo*. He then offered the fresh *guarapo* as a drink (with or without rum) to interested customers. The man was an exceptionally dark Afro-Cuban, which led me to wonder about the racial make-up of Cubans.

"Are Afro-Cubans in the minority or majority? I haven't seen very many Black people here yet," I asked Julian, rather bluntly.

"Hmm, that's a good question," replied Julian, who didn't mind answering straightforward questions. "About two-thirds of the inhabitants here are of European descent, another twenty percent are mixed race and ten or fifteen percent are of more or less pure Black African heritage. But you don't find the same proportion everywhere: there are only a few dark-skinned people in the west – around Vinales, for example – but their proportion is much, much higher in places like Santiago in the east. I know that because I wrote a brochure on Cuba for Brigham Young University once and I had to look it up."

"So is there much prejudice against people of color in Cuba?"

"Officially, no. And certainly not in school or in politics. But there is definitely social prejudice against very dark-skinned people. In our town there is a young woman – she is Caucasian – and this girl is quite in love with our young pastor, who is Black. He would like to marry her, too, but the girl's mother is mortally opposed to such a marriage. Mortally. She told her daughter, 'If you marry him I will starve myself to death,' and to underline her words she stopped eating for a whole month and lost twenty-five kilos – about fifty pounds. Imagine! She looked like a skeleton compared to before. So this scared her daughter and it has prevented the marriage so far."

The day after our arduous and overheated trek to and from the cemetery, Julian suggested taking a city bus instead of walking to the old town. So we lined up at the bus stop on La Rampa, amongst dozens of people in clean and freshly pressed clothes, waiting for the P05 bus to take them to work. When the bus finally came, we all filed past the driver, depositing ridiculously low fares of about two cents on the way by. The seats were already full before the bus arrived, so what we were doing was just filling up the aisle, which was getting more and more packed. By the time the driver closed the doors on the last few people desirous of traveling with us, nobody in the bus was worried about falling over. They were, rather, worried about breathing, and I was among the most worried. I have never felt more squashed, not in rush-hour subways in New York, not in mountain cable cars in Switzerland. Before getting on the bus, Julian had warned me not to speak to him in English as, once again, buses are heavily subsidized, and other passengers might feel that I was taking the place of a more legitimate user. Now there was definitely no danger of giving myself away because I could barely breathe, let alone converse with Julian. Luckily, all passengers were bound for the old town, so we all stood in the aisle like vertical anchovies, a solid mass of swaying, shallow-breathing humanity, praying that we'd be able to get off when the time came.

When the bus finally spat us out near the Plaza de Armas, Julian and I just stood there for a few moments, re-expanding our lungs and enjoying the fresh air. Then we meandered through several small street-corner parks, shady and green with tall palms, hanging vines and flowers, where gray-haired men chatted animatedly over a game of chess, toddlers chased pigeons or slept in their strollers, and mothers and grandmothers sat on benches, conversing in animated tones. One of these parks was dedicated to the German scientist and explorer Alexander von Humboldt, who'd lived in a nearby house while carrying out research in Cuba in 1800 and 1804. Like so many others, he was fascinated by the island and its particular flora and fauna, and believed that the people of Cuba had a promising future.

We were now back on Obispo Street and just couldn't resist the temptation to stroll its length once more. There were a number of places we had failed to investigate on the first day: there was ETECSA, the Cuban telephone company and provider of internet connections for tourists. There were two government-run bookshops that just possibly had a new book on José Marti for Julian. There was Ambos Mundos, the hotel that Hemingway had lived in when writing For Whom The Bell Tolls. There were those ornate and colorful ceramic street signs that I'd forgotten to photograph on the first day. There were bicitaxis and horse-drawn buggies plying the side-streets. There was a working nineteenth-century pharmacy, complete with mahogany counters and hundreds of phials and porcelain apothecary jars, still dispensing medications and teas.

"Oh look," said Julian pointing to the top of a large stately building in the distance. "There's the Capitolio, where our conference will be held tomorrow."

"Really? Inside that building?" I gulped, my heart suddenly pounding.

"Yes, of course. ANGLO is a very important academic organization, and that's the headquarters of the Cuban Academy of Science."

"But it really looks just like the US Capitol building."

"Yes, yes. It was designed to look like that. The Cuban parliament used to meet there before the revolution."

Just as Julian mentioned Castro's revolution, my eye fell on two dachshunds dressed as guerrilla fighters, wearing miniature camouflage fatigues, Che Guevara berets and sunglasses. They had been perched on the seat and in the basket of a bicycle by their owner, who was no doubt hoping I would take their picture so that he could ask me for money. I couldn't help giggling a little, but soon stopped, filled with a mixture of emotions: I worried that I or the man might be charged with counter-revolutionary disrespect, but I also felt sorry for the dogs' humiliation.

"Julian," I said as we walked on, "do you see those dogs as a parody of revolutionaries?"

"Heh, heh, I see what you mean – well, it's a delicate question," he answered. "If you're ehm a fervent revolutionary, you don't see it as a parody, you see it as 'Everybody's for the revolution.' But, yes, if you have doubts about the revolution, you probably see it as a parody. But nobody objects, because everybody wants to give the impression of being pro-revolution. Clever, no?"

***

After another tasty lunch at La Marina, we took the birdcage elevator to the roof of the Ambos Mundos hotel and had a coffee, enjoying the spectacular view over Havana harbor.

"I'd forgotten that Havana's a port," I said. "It would be perfect for cruise ships to visit. They'd be docked right in the old town."

"Oh, they already come – a few anyway. From Russia and Scandinavia… and Canada, too, I think."

"Yes, but wait till the American tourists start coming – then you'll really see some tourist development."

"That's what we are a bit afraid of – that the Americans want to develop us according to their ehm…"

"Do you mean in their image?"

"Yes – I mean that they will try to make Cuba like,… like Disneyland."

"Oh no, that would be terrible, wouldn't it?" We

reviewed our separate visions of an Americanized Cuba for a moment. Then I remembered something I'd been wanting to ask Julian.

"You know, when we walk down the street here, I never see anyone chewing gum. Is gum against the law or…?"

"No, no," he laughed. "Chewing gum – we call it *chiclé* – is permitted of course, but no one can afford it. And as no one buys it, it is practically not sold."

"And what about graffiti and posters on the walls? Are they banned? I haven't seen any – or maybe just a little graffiti so far."

"You are very good at observing things! The reason we have no – or almost no – posters is because of lack of paper. This is due to the US embargo. And as for, ehm, graffiti, it does exist, but it is almost always pro-government and it is always on outdoor walls, in a very visible place. You will see it."

I mulled this over, concluding that a shortage of paper was very convenient for the Castro regime. With no paper for flyers, no cell phones and very restricted internet access, it would be fairly difficult to organize political opposition.

"Will we take the bus back to Vedado – what do you think?" ventured Julian, probably worried that I'd suggest walking back.

"Fine with me," I said. "It probably won't be as crowded now."

So we looked for and found the nearest P05 bus stop, where seven or eight people were already standing in the hot sunshine or leaning against buildings in the shade, all obviously waiting for the bus.

"*Quien es el ultimo*?" inquired Julian in a public voice, and a man standing across the quiet street half raised his hand.

"What was that about?" I asked.

"When you wait for the bus you have to know who is the last person in line. That's the person you're behind when the bus comes."

And sure enough, when another would-be passenger arrived a moment later, he addressed a "*Quien es el ultimo*?" to the scattered queue. Julian said "*Aqui*" and raised his hand slightly.

This reminded me of the queuing I'd experienced when Julian and I had gone to a Canadian movie the previous evening. Havana has a number of large, old-fashioned cinemas, which are used for the annual international film festival. With subsidized tickets in hand, we joined a huge, but surprisingly orderly, queue of several hundred people, who calmly filed into the vast cinema, four abreast, without pushing, raising their voices or grabbing the best seats. Cuban waiting lines were impressive examples of cooperative civil behavior.

When our bus finally came, scattered bystanders quickly transformed themselves into an orderly queue. This time the driver leaned out the bus door and collected our fares in his hand, directing us to the back door, where he assured us there was plenty of room. Unfortunately, he was wrong.

We hadn't been aboard long, when a very old woman seated near my tiny patch of aisle space leaned forward against the seat in front of her and groaned a few words. She was obviously not feeling well. Instead of ignoring her, as would probably have happened in Zurich, about five passengers immediately showed concern and asked questions. At the next stop, the woman was virtually carried off the bus and helped to sit down on nearby steps by two of the passengers, who remained with her. I was touched and impressed.

———— ••• ————

As I lay in bed that evening, the sights and sounds of the day flashing through my head, I reflected on the understanding of Cuban society that was evolving in my mind. Cubans are in some ways unique; in terms of cash, they live on well under $1 a day, like the poorest people in the world. However, because of subsidies and the high level of education and medical care, they have a standard of living similar to that in many areas of southern Europe. What's more, and despite the US embargo, they are probably better informed about the rest of the world than people in many Western countries. Julian was well up on international politics, scientific developments, recent films, popular Western TV shows, and issues like global warming. In social domains I found Cubans to be more advanced than most Westerners, such as their public civility in waiting lines at cinemas and bus stops, or their willingness to help each other spontaneously in the street. Many young Cubans also volunteer for service abroad in a sort of Cuban Medical Corps that helps the poor and distressed in Latin America and Africa. This was all highly admirable, and something that Westerners usually hear nothing about. However, I was also starting to become aware of regime control. For example, the way perpetual shortages – of paper, water, transport, electricity and certain foods – kept Cubans' minds focused on coping with scarcity instead of thinking about politics. Did the government deliberately allow these shortages to persist? The US embargo was publicly blamed for all Cuba's economic problems, but this could not possibly be true. And there was absolutely no public space for political opposition. My understanding of Cuban society had taken a leap forward in just a few days, but I still had only a vague idea of what it felt like to be a Cuban in Cuba. I hoped to find out more at the English teachers' conference.

6
THE CUBAN ENGLISH
TEACHERS' CONFERENCE

OMETHING HAD CHANGED. I PEERED at the
horizon between the slats of my bedroom shutters:
thick gray clouds were gathering and the usually
tranquil Atlantic had developed whitecaps. Was the
summery December weather about to desert us, just
when I was starting to take it for granted? It was the
first day of the English teachers' conference, and I was
looking forward finally to meeting some other Cubans
and learning more about life in Cuba.

On its first day, the ANGLO conference was scheduled
to take place in the afternoon only. Julian and I arrived
well ahead of noon and discovered that the Cuban
Capitolio was much easier to get into than its American
namesake. We simply walked unchallenged up the broad,
dizzying steps and entered the building by its massive
front door. The reason for this easy access was that the
Cuban parliament no longer met there; it had moved to
a different location after the revolution of 1959, and the

Capitolio had been handed over to the Cuban Academy of Science.

We looked around the cavernous first floor lobby, but only found a hand-written sign informing us that the ANGLO conference was being held on the second floor, so we staggered up another steep marble staircase. The gallery at the top of the stairs took the rest of my breath away. It was a grand hallway, perhaps three-hundred-feet long, with light streaming in from one side through tall glass doors that opened onto a balcony. The hallway was made entirely of marble, with an ornate ceiling and polished inlaid floors that were so shiny, they reflected the room's gold and marble ornaments like mirrors.

We had arrived far too early for the opening session, but signs of a registration area were already evident. Julian went off to speak to a colleague at one side of the vast hall and I moved towards the registration desk, hoping to pick up handouts, plus maybe a program and a name badge, as one does at such conferences. I stepped up to the desk. "Hello." I said cheerily, "My name is Heather Murray and I am registered as a keynote speaker." The young woman I was addressing, who was probably a university student who'd been "volunteered" for the job by her English teacher, smiled shyly and searched for my name on a list, then collected some papers and handed them to me, saying:

"Yes, here the badge and program for you. But, sorry, you ehm you have not yet pay the register fee. Please can you go to the Treasurer Mrs. Hernandez – she is sitting there (indicating a woman across the room)?" This puzzled me.

"Registration fees for guest speakers?" I muttered to myself, frowning, as I crossed the marbled hall. I had never heard of speakers having to pay a registration fee; they were supposed to be the drawing cards, for heaven's sake! Wrong again. The seventy-CUC registration fee was *only* for guest speakers. Who else could possibly afford it? I should have thought about that before, but I didn't: ordinary Cubans, with salaries under twenty-five CUCs a month, would never have been able to pay what amounted to three months' salary to attend a conference. The Cuban members were all paying a much lower fee, and the three guest speakers, who had either paid their own way to Cuba or been sponsored by a British publisher or the British Council, were precisely the ones who had to pay the higher fee, because this was needed to cover conference expenses.

Luckily I had the seventy CUCs on me and handed them over to Mrs. Hernandez. Inwardly smoldering with righteous indignation, I tried to slip on the mask of a blasé keynote speaker. When she had carefully put my money away in what looked a lot like her own wallet, Mrs. Hernandez said:

"There will be a conference dinner for the ANGLO board and especially invited guests, including the conference speakers, on the last day of the conference. Would you like to come?"

"Oh, that's nice. Thank you," I said, shifting facial gears to a gracious smile.

"I'm glad you can come," she said, also donning a frozen smile, "the participation fee for the dinner is ten CUCs."

Were they insulting me on purpose? Did they fleece all guest speakers like this? When I recovered my composure, I said:

"Can I just check with Julian before paying? I have to ask him what we're doing on the last day of the conference. I'm his guest, you know." Brimming with a chaos of feelings, I went to look for Julian, still smarting from their audacity in asking me to fund both the conference *and* the dinner. When I finally spotted him in the rapidly filling lobby, he was already looking for me. Mrs. Hernandez' envoy had found him first.

"Heather, you have to attend the conference dinner on Saturday afternoon," he explained. "I'm going, you know – I always am invited – and if you don't pay your ten CUCs they will not be able to have it. They need the money for buying the food." Without a word, I returned to Mrs. Hernandez, who was waiting, crocodile-like, at her table.

Now, with hindsight, having seen how strapped the Cuban economy is, and how little money each person lives on, it seems perfectly logical that the organizers needed to extract money from foreign participants to be able to stage the conference and conference dinner, but on that first day of acquaintance with Cuban financial reality I felt exploited. Nor could I get my mind around the fact that a conference with virtually no financial support was being held in such a marvelously ornate building. But that was Cuba: a beggar dressed in silks and gold inherited from times past.

After the shake-down start, my first ANGLO conference day became more like other conferences I had attended. Strangers mingled and chatted, or stood shyly on the sidelines, seemingly engrossed in their program, waiting for the proceedings to start. Julian introduced me to members of the ANGLO board, with whom he seemed to be on the best of terms. This assured me a very warm welcome and permitted me to experience Cuban introduction protocol: when I met someone new I was supposed to shake men's hands, but was required to kiss women on the cheek at our very first meeting. I was familiar with kissing people on both cheeks from living in Europe for nearly forty years, but these Cuban kisses were not only distributed to both cheeks, but planted three times per cheek in rapid succession with a mch-mch-mch sound, as if calling an animal. This took some getting used to – and I never really managed the mch, mch, mch – but since I met a great many female teachers, I became inured to being well and truly kissed.

I had brought with me to the conference my gift of fifty Swiss chocolate bars, which I'd intended to give to conference participants "from the English teachers of Switzerland". Feeling unsure about how to accomplish this major step in international understanding by myself, I gave the whole box of bars to the wife of ANGLO's president – after duly kissing her in the approved manner – and asked her to make sure they were distributed at some point. She was a woman who obviously liked her food, so I had misgivings as soon as the box left my hands.

When the conference finally got under way, more than a hundred ANGLO members and guests found ourselves seated in a large, ornate legislative chamber with air-conditioning cold enough to keep meat for days. No one seemed to know how to turn it off, so we just had to sit and shiver. Apart from short opening speeches, introductions and program announcements, the only talk on the first day was a plenary on developing a new English curriculum, delivered by a female professor of English from a sports college in central Cuba. The content of the presentation was neither novel nor fascinating, but the style of delivery was rather remarkable: the woman just stood up without notes, faced the audience from where she was sitting, and proceeded to deliver a one-hour talk in English from memory, without slides or other illustrations. When she started, Julian leaned towards me and muttered grimly through his teeth: "She already gave this talk at another ANGLO meeting." The audience listened politely I thought (considering that they were freezing and bored), but there were only one or two questions at the end. The rather brief first day was then adjourned and we were told that the next two days would be spent on the premises of a technical college in Habana Centro. This was when I realized I wouldn't have to stand up in front of the group in these rather terrifying marbled halls, but would be giving my talk in the more familiar surroundings of a college.

"Hah!" commented Julian, "ANGLO always used to offer a conference aperitif on the first evening at a Havana hotel or at the Havana Club distillery, but I think this year there must be no money. The President told me that the British Council gave ANGLO less money this year and that Canada has withdrawn its funding completely."

"Well 2008 has been a tough year financially in most countries," I said.

"Yes, but with ANGLO I wonder where will it end. We can't exist without subsidies from other countries." I was beginning to get the picture.

The atmosphere was one of going from bad to worse: what new straits would the future hold as a result of the financial crisis? Even the skies over Havana hung leaden and brooding when we emerged from the conference. Julian and I took a taxi back to Vedado and then went our separate ways. I wanted to wash my hair when the water came on at six-thirty, and otherwise prepare for the next day's performance. Julian had plans to meet up with his friend Felix in the evening.

———————

The day of my talk dawned sunny and clear. I was up at six, rehearsing parts of it mentally and looking through the overhead transparencies that I'd made in case there was no computer for my PowerPoint slides. The speaker of the previous day had had no visual aids, I reflected. Maybe no equipment would be available at all; at least I had enough multi-paged handouts for 120 people. I had slept badly, but had been able to wash my hair the night before, and sort out my clothes for my moment of glory.

Magdalena didn't usually get up till about half-past seven, so I had a quiet breakfast by myself. Then I put on the outfit I'd been saving to wear for the big day, gathered up the heavy pile of handouts I had been instructed by ANGLO to bring with me (Speakers must bring all handouts with them. There are no facilities for copying at the conference site.) and carefully walked down the emergency stairs from the tenth floor in high-heeled sandals. My old enemy, the elevator, was not going to get me today of all days.

Julian was already waiting on the front steps, as usual.

"Good morning, Heather!" he beamed. "Well, and how did you sleep last night?"

I lied that I had slept very well and did not mention that I'd already been up for two hours.

"At least the weather is supporting you," he commented. "It is much cooler today, so people will be wide awake." The weather had indeed changed from blustery cloud to cool, bright sunshine.

We took a taxi to the conference venue and were there by 8.15, only to discover that, due to another activity, the auditorium would not be accessible until 9.30, the time when I was supposed to be starting my talk. This did not faze Julian in the slightest; it seemed as if he was used to all kinds of last-minute difficulties like this. We filled in the time walking round and round the block and talking about architecture, life, families – whatever Julian could think of to keep me from getting nervous. Finally, we were allowed to enter the auditorium along with everybody else. I handed my memory stick to a technician, who quickly and efficiently set up my slides on a laptop. Meanwhile the school principal had picked up the microphone from the front desk and started welcoming the audience of ANGLO members in an off-the-cuff speech. Like every other Cuban I have observed with a microphone, whether five-year-old, primary school teacher or Fidel himself, he was not at a loss for words. That set the tone for me, and when my turn came I grabbed the mike like an old pro and never looked back. It was the most relaxed talk I have ever given. The time flew by, my slides flowed and I got a big round of applause at the end. Strangers came up afterwards and said how much they had enjoyed it. It was all highly gratifying, but what made me happiest of all was Julian's reaction.

"Well," he murmured as I sat down next to him in the front row after the break that followed my talk, "that was excellent."

"Really?" I couldn't believe it.

"Oh sure, sure. Everybody is congratulating me for bringing you to the conference."

The two other guest speakers, both from Britain, had the speaking slots after mine. Then came lunch – a brief, informal affair, consisting of processed cheese sandwiches, juice and coffee, all consumed standing up. Given the virtually non-existent financial resources, it was pretty good.

Participants kept on mingling and chatting with each other. There were two main topics of conversation. One was recent hurricane damage caused by the three disastrous storms that had struck Cuba in October and November 2008. Hundreds of houses had been washed away, roofs lifted, palm trees decapitated. Despite the damage, and despite many casualties elsewhere in the Caribbean, no Cuban had been killed. Not one. The other topic was what is called the "financial crisis" in the West. In Cuba, where people live in a state of permanent financial crisis, the latest news was not about banks collapsing, but about western publishers and governments withdrawing financial aid and discontinuing gifts of textbooks and other materials.

———— •••• ————

Teachers of English from universities all over Cuba attended the conference. Many of them approached me with questions about my talk and exchanged email addresses with me. Some even gave me small presents. For example, Ysenadi, a charming young "Generation Y" lecturer from Pinar del Rio province, gave me a small embroidered Cuban flag to pin on my blouse, and made me promise to write him an email when I got back to Switzerland. Eduardo, who taught English at the University of Santiago, gave me a three-peso note with a picture of Che on it as a souvenir. He also wanted to start exchanging emails and pressed his homemade visiting card into my hand. I was finally meeting lots of Cubans. Would this lead to invitations to visit their home universities, I wondered?

When Julian saw all the attention I was getting, he smiled sardonically and raised one eyebrow.

"Yes, yes, they all want contact with someone in the outside world."

"What do you mean 'outside world'?" I asked.

"Just anywhere outside Cuba. It can be helpful for Cubans to have friends in other countries."

"How could it be helpful?"

"Well, their new friends might send things, like articles or books, or they might send an invitation to visit or even arrange a scholarship. You know, it's sometimes possible for us to leave Cuba for a course or a conference if we are invited…"

"Is that how you got to attend your course in Edinburgh?" I asked. "Were you invited by a friend?"

"No, no. I won a British Council scholarship. But, I mean, it's just a possibility that keeps people from," he lowered his voice, "*feeling trapped on this island.*"

I started to see the overtures of the Cuban conference participants in a somewhat different light. Did Julian want me to invite him to Switzerland, I wondered? I would have to ask him later when we were alone.

At the afternoon coffee break I happened to be standing next to a middle-aged member of the ANGLO board who had a telegenic face and a gorgeously suave announcer's voice. He had done some of the introductions at the opening session, but I couldn't remember exactly what his function was in the organization, so I used that as an opener.

"I'm sorry, I don't remember your name from yesterday, but your voice is unforgettable – and your English is remarkable. You sound like an American."

"Thank you," he lowered his eyes modestly, but had obviously heard this many times before. "Well, it's because I *am* partly American, although I've spent my whole life in Cuba. My name is George Perez. My mother was American, so that's how I learned English… and then I used my English to get a job with Cuban radio and TV. I used to read the news in English for Cuban International Radio and then got involved in an English-for-schools TV project. That's why I'm a member of ANGLO."

"Hmm. Interesting," I replied. "I would have

guessed that learning English is not a top priority for Cuban schools."

"Heh heh. I understand why you think that. The US is really unpopular because of the embargo, the *bloqueo* as they call it here, which has made people's lives just miserable. But there are lots of other associations with the English language that do not involve the US. There's Canada, which sends us so many things: two million tourists, trucks, school buses, cows, teachers, school supplies… Then there's the rest of the Caribbean: Jamaica, Trinidad and Tobago, Barbados, Antigua, Grenada and so on. We do a lot of university exchanges with them. And finally there's the rest of the world, where English is pretty much *the* international language. No, no; parents are realistic about the usefulness of English and they want their children to learn it."

"Has it ever been hard for you personally," I asked, "living with American roots here in Cuba?"

"No, not really. I mean Cuba is my home. My friends and family are here and I don't feel any need to go to the US, since I never knew it. It was probably harder for my mom – when she was alive. Not seeing her parents and relatives and things like that."

I decided to play my naïve card now. "Have you ever interviewed somebody like Castro in English for the radio?" I ventured.

His smile waned in the uncomfortable pause. "Oh no. I'm not a reporter – I'm a newsreader. I don't do interviews – just read scripts and news bulletins, so, I mean, I wouldn't uh be asked to do anything like that."

"Sure, yeah, I see," I nodded understandingly. But he

had already noticed someone across the room he had to talk to, excused himself with a tiny bow and left my side before I could come up with another indelicate question. It was indeed interesting to see how my question had affected him. This made me reflect on the conversations, in both Spanish and English, that I'd overheard during the lunch break. There was never a hint of complaint about a lack of Cuban government funding, never the slightest whisper of the name Castro. Either the two were taken for granted, or this was something you didn't discuss in public.

After the three plenary talks on the second day, the conference broke up into a series of parallel workshops led by about twenty different ANGLO members. These focused on Canadian, British and Caribbean (with no mention of US) literature, on teaching English for special purposes, like aviation, sports, medicine and technology, and English teacher training programs in the various universities. ANGLO members were enthusiastic workshop attenders, keen to learn anything new that they could take home and put into practice.

I felt proud that my talk had been so practical, focusing as it did on how teachers could use free lists of academic vocabulary from the internet to help their students improve their reading and writing in English. That was, until I talked a little more to Ysenadi, the lecturer from Pinar del Río. He had asked me for extra copies of my handout, which unfortunately had run out after my talk. "I'm sorry there aren't any left, but don't worry," I said, "you can just look it all up on the internet. It's on my website – I can give you the internet address and you can just download it from there and print it out." He gave me a wan smile and said, "Yes, thank you." A while later, Julian located me and asked for an extra copy of my handouts for a friend from Santa Clara who'd missed the talk. Again, I explained and said I'd give him the address of my website.

"Hmm," he said, "it's not so easy to get things from the internet."

"You have email at the university, don't you?" I reminded him.

"Yes, we have email addresses at the university, that's right, but it's imposs... – well it's very difficult to go to internet websites outside Cuba." He said this with some embarrassment.

I had read that personal computers were not available for private citizens, and that there was also very tight control of cell phones (virtually none visible on the street), but I hadn't realized that ordinary Cubans weren't free to surf the internet or even just download useful information from a website. That explained why the receptionist took down my passport details when I used the internet to check my email at the state-run telecommunications office. The government probably wanted to know who was accessing the internet.

On the third and final day, after the last workshops had finished, the conference was brought to a close by a reliably boring annual general meeting of ANGLO members. Motivation to attend the business meeting increased, however, when it was announced that there would be a prize-drawing with my Swiss chocolate bars as prizes. Instead of using a winner-take-all model, the wise president's wife had opened the box of fifty individually wrapped chocolate bars and re-packaged them in bundles of five, thus creating a number of prizes, each containing enough chocolate to make a Cuban family happy. The tears of joy when the chocolate prizes were awarded made me feel mean for not bringing two hundred bars. I was curious, though, to see whether ten bundles had been made or whether some of the chocolate had been held back. Sure enough, there were only five or six tombola winners, leaving at least twenty bars unaccounted for. Had they been confiscated for private use?

It was time to say goodbye to many of the people I'd met at the conference. I felt very happy about the way things had gone with my talk and with meeting lots of Cubans, but also slightly disappointed that I had failed to receive even one invitation to visit another part of Cuba. People had plied me with small gifts and pressed their university email addresses upon me, but no one had offered to show me around their hometown of Camaguey or Las Tunas, Santiago or Pinar del Rio. Was this because they didn't want to be seen with me, because they were afraid of incurring expenses or because they were just too busy? It was difficult to know. And I couldn't even ask Julian. He, too, had been unmistakably reticent about meeting me when I had booked a tour for the following week that included his hometown of Santa Clara. The conference had not provided a means to explore other parts of Cuba, but it had provided a number of insights into the difficulties of Cuban life.

7
HASTA LA VISTA

IRECTLY AFTER CONFERENCE ADJOURNMENT we were to go to the post-conference dinner with the ANGLO bigwigs in Nuevo Vedado, the once-posh embassy suburb on the far side of Magdalena's neighborhood. As I was a major contributor to the dinner fund, I didn't want to miss it. I extricated myself from the firm handclasp of a would-be Cuban pen-pal, latched onto Julian's arm and dashed out through the main doors of the college, where we hailed a passing taxi. Luckily, Julian knew the address.

The house that was our destination belonged to Muriel, an ANGLO member whose family had lived in it since pre-revolution days. A bilingual Cuban of Irish descent, she'd taught English at a Havana college, but was now retired. I suspected she was on the ANGLO board for the sole purpose of providing a classy venue for the conference dinner. Her white stucco villa was set back from the street, between hedged front and back yards, the latter also featuring a white-tiled swimming pool sunk into the ground. Judging from the debris and dried leaves in it, though, the pool was not in use.

When we arrived, about twenty of the ANGLO elite were already strewn about the back garden and spacious living room, which were connected by French doors reminiscent of the Cuban consulate in Bern. They were drinking rum and cola and chatting in small groups. A grizzled black Labrador made the rounds, hoping for a dropped cracker or a scratch behind the ear.

Julian went outside to chat with old friends, while I fell into conversation with Marilyn, an American woman who had been living and teaching English in Cuba for the past twenty years. She had long, silver-threaded dark hair and a friendly face, but looked somehow tired and undernourished. How did she, an American, come to be working in Cuba, I wanted to know.

"Oh well, that was a long time ago – in the eighties," she answered. "I guess it was a sort of romantic dream to come to the land of Che and experience the revolution firsthand. First of all, it wasn't easy to get here. I had to go to Mexico and get a ticket and a visa for Cuba from there. Then, when I got here, I didn't know exactly where to look for a job. *Tons* of regulations and permits and checks. And then, finally, I made friends with people who worked at the University of Havana, and they helped me get into the English department."

"So you got a university job right away? That's pretty good."

"Well, not really. I was hired as a conversation tutor – not allowed to teach literature, not allowed to teach grammar – just allowed to run conversation classes. And was paid accordingly. I could not *believe* the salaries people were earning when I arrived. Fifteen dollars a month! Starvation wages."

"But could you live on that with the subsidized food and everything?"

"No way. Well… I could almost live on it if I shared a room in a student apartment, walked everywhere and didn't eat anything but bread and potatoes. But I started to do translations and give private lessons on the side, and earned money that way. But then things got worse. Even bread was scarce in the nineties when the USSR fell apart."

"So why did you stay here when things were going from bad to worse?"

"Partly for love. Yeah, I met this Cuban ballet dancer – *really* handsome and *really* nice. I mean, it was love, right? And then there was also this great feeling of solidarity here because of the US boycott. I never felt that before. Everybody was helping each other – with food, with medicine, with fixing things, right? It just felt like a great time to be alive and be here – y'know what I mean? – and then one thing led to another and, well… here I still am."

I said I could imagine that it felt good to be part of a special time like that. "Is there the same feeling of solidarity today?" I asked.

"Nope, not at all," she scoffed. "People are a lot less open nowadays – more secretive. They don't want you to know they have relatives in Florida, sending them money."

I mentioned how friendly some ANGLO members were at the conference with their little presents and email addresses, but how it surprised me that they didn't invite me to visit them at their universities.

"Oh no, no, they won't do anything like that," she said. "They're embarrassed by how cramped and dilapidated their houses are. They can actually watch American TV series now – and they see how westerners live, which makes them, like, more aware of how little they have here by comparison. Nope, no way. They'll never invite somebody like you to visit them at home."

———————————

I continued looking around the villa while the other guests chatted away, indoors and out. On the far side of the living room, a tall bookcase with glass doors beckoned. The embossed leather covers and titles in Spanish and English indicated that the books had been bought in other times, when money was more plentiful. The pale pink wallpaper with its faded pattern of magnolias and exotic birds linked by golden tendrils, also spoke of a more prosperous era; the cracked and crumbling plaster spoke of now.

A peek into the steamy kitchen revealed Muriel, her glasses shifted to her forehead, directing a team of four local women especially hired for the occasion. They had headscarves on and business-like aprons, and were doing their best to cook the conference feast, which consisted of roast pork, rice and black beans, yucca, *congris*, green beans, tomato salad and more. For dessert there was a huge, professionally produced cake sitting on the sideboard, its decoration thanking the ANGLO board for another year of hard work. It was a thank you from the board members to themselves; there would be a lot left over to take home afterwards.

When it was ready, the meal was served as a buffet and savored by one and all in reverent semi-silence. Toasts of warm cola were drunk to visitors, the board and old friendships. Finally, the cake was brought out in all its flaming glory, followed by the solution to the mystery of the missing Swiss chocolate bars: each person present was given a bar with their coffee, thus confirming the wisdom of the ANGLO president's wife.

Julian and I left the conference feast as soon as dessert and propriety permitted. He had a ticket for the midnight bus back to Santa Clara, where he had to teach a Bible class the following morning. Now he wanted to shower and pack before coming over to Magdalena's to say goodbye.

I thought I'd take a shower, too, when I got home. Luckily there was still some Saturday-morning water in the cistern, because the mains water was off all evening.

"No, no, there's never water on Saturday evening," Magdalena asserted, as if it were a God-given law. It seemed strange to me that there was no running water in Havana on Saturday evenings, when people might want to freshen up before going out for the evening. Did people go out unwashed? Or did they clean up in the morning and then try to stay fresh all day?

In Cuba, the veil of dusk always fell at some indefinable point between six and seven. I was aware of the sun's disc being swallowed by the sea out my bedroom window and hardly noticed when the fishing boats became points of light on the dark ocean. Magdalena knocked on my bedroom door to offer me what she called *poudeen,* i.e. pudding, which was a slice of ultra-firm flan. So I went into the kitchen and sat down with her, prepared to be quizzed on the day's proceedings.

What did we do at the conference today, she wanted to know. Well, it was the last day and we had a big dinner, I replied as I stuffed another spoonful of flan into my mouth. Was the dinner good? Yes, delicious: roast pork and rice and beans and other things.

"*Ah si, comida criolla,*" she confirmed.

Where was the dinner – in a restaurant?

No, in a house in Nuevo Vedado.

Aha, was the house pretty?

Yes, quite pretty. It was white with green trim and had a swimming pool without water.

Ah well, it's winter now, Magdalena said.

Yes, but I think the pool never has water in it, I said.

Everything is getting worse, she commented with mild melancholy, as she shook her head.

I told her about talking to George Perez from Cuban radio and TV.

Oh yes, she said, she had seen him on television; he was a nice man, but unfortunately married to a niece of Castro's.

I almost choked on my last bite of *poudeen.* "His wife's a Castro?"

Oh yes, she said ominously, there are lots of Castros in Cuba, but it's not always a good idea to marry them.

———————

Julian came by to pick me up for a farewell drink at the

Nacional. He left his small suitcase in my room and we made our way down to the street, crossing towards the beckoning hotel lights. The night breeze was still balmy. They might call this winter, but to me it was like a warm evening in June. We strolled through the lobby and out the back of the hotel to the portico, where we settled into one of the thick-cushioned rattan couches, just in time to observe a full moon drop from behind a band of cloud.

"Julian, did you order this moon for our last evening together?" I teased.

"No, I… heh heh… I mean yes, of course. It's beautiful the way it makes lines on the sea."

"Mhm, those are called moonbeams, I think. Some people believe that you can travel across the sea on moonbeams."

"Travel on moonbeams?"

"Yes, where would you go if you could travel anywhere?"

"To Spain… and Australia… maybe Chile…"

As we waited to order drinks from the portico waiter, a trio of hotel musicians – guitar, flute and bongos – appeared and serenaded us for several minutes with their version of *Guantanamera*. This embarrassed me a little, but didn't seem to bother Julian in the slightest; in fact he sang along with the first verse.

When the trio had wandered on to the next couch he said: "Well, it's a pity I have to work the whole week coming. But I talked to our pastor on the phone this evening and told him I won't come to church next Sunday, so I can come back to Havana and spend it with you before you leave. I have already booked the ticket, too."

"That's wonderful – that's so nice of you," I said, starting to realize what a huge effort this was for him. "I really love seeing the sights and just walking around Havana with you. It's much more memorable than doing it alone."

"Well, next week you will see more of Cuba. You have your two tours – to Vinales and then to Central Cuba – Trinidad and so on. I hope you will be careful and not do anything dangerous."

"Like what?"

"Well, like walking alone in the night."

"No, I won't do that. I promise. But, I mean, why isn't it safe? I see guards or people who look like police on lots of corners."

"Yes, but they are not there for *you*."

By this time Julian and I had slipped further down into our well-cushioned couch. We were feeling relaxed. Julian lowered his voice.

"You know, the ehm the Commander-in-Chief – you know who I mean? – the C-in-C? Well, he hates prostitution and gambling and other capitalist crimes, so the police are standing on corners to guard us against that."

"The C-in-C sounds like a strict Presbyterian."

"Heh heh. Well, prostitution is a symbol of the bad old days under Batista, so of course he has to be against it. And... do you know what José Marti said? He said, 'Others... go to bed with their mistresses, but I, I go to bed with my ideas.' And I think that's true for the C-in-C, too."

"But I think he has ten children, even if he's not married, right?"

"Yes, that's true! He has mistresses *and* ideas." He laughed some more, enjoying our mildly subversive joke.

By this time the moon was huge, lighting everything. I felt as if I was sitting on a movie set, so I lowered my voice to a murmur.

"I think Cuban life has been strongly influenced by the C-in-C's decisions, hasn't it?" I ventured. "Did the C-in-C affect your life much?"

"Oh, completely. For example, when I finished the university I joined the ministry of education and became a school inspector. I observed English teachers and inspected programs for the government – yes, I traveled all over Cuba then: Pinar del Rio, Trinidad, Santiago... Many, many country schools too, because you know the C-in-C decided to remove all the high school students from the cities, where they were supposed to be exposed to bad influences, and sent them to the country, where they would learn to ehm to appreciate the work of the *campesinos* and live in innocence, so-called. So new high schools were built in the country and teenagers were taken away from their families in the city and lived together in boarding schools. You can imagine what happened! Well, maybe they *did* learn to appreciate the work of the *campesinos*, because – you know – cutting sugar cane is hard work, hot work, but mostly it was just a total, total chaos. Complete. And the quality of education suffered because of that. It was nearly impossible to motivate English teachers who were used to cities for life in the countryside. But anyway, it was just an idea and ideas come and go with the C-in-C. The problem is that nobody wants to be the first one to tell him his idea is bad, so projects fail for a long time before they are stopped. Yes, the revolution had a really big influence on my life."

"Is that why you stopped working in the education ministry?"

"Not only. I was getting tired of the traveling. And most of all, I had a problem with the spiritual side. I couldn't express my religious ideas, which were becoming more important to me. So I found a job teaching medical students at the university in Santa Clara, where I could ehm be myself, you know? So now I can stay at home and be with the family – help with my mother, who's quite... she's over ninety – see some good friends, and well...."

"Santa Clara's not *that* small, is it?"

"No, but sometimes I still miss Havana, because of course Santa Clara is not Havana – there is practically nothing to do in the evening – but fundamentally I think I made the right decision."

"Oh listen, listen," Julian whispered after a brief pause, "they are playing my favorite song. I love Frank Sinatra." The little trio, who had passed by our couch at least twice in the meantime, were fulfilling another guest's request by playing Sinatra's *My Way*. Julian, who has a beautifully rich tenor voice, sang along with the music:

> For what is a man, what has he got?
> If not himself, then he has naught.
> To say the things he truly feels;
> And not the words of one who kneels.
> The record da, da-da da-da
> And did it my way.

"How on earth do you know all those words?" I asked, truly amazed.

"Someone gave me a Frank Sinatra record once and I memorized everything."

Conversation gave way to silence once again, with one of us possibly reflecting on Sinatra's words and the other thinking about how one powerful person can irrevocably shape others' lives.

"Well, Heather," said Julian finally, "this has been a very interesting week and I have had a wonderful time, thanks to you. I knew a lot about you from your letters and emails, but I didn't know about your sense of humor and your quiet, understanding way."

In situations like this, I get embarrassed and am not very good at saying what I feel, so I just said, "I've had a wonderful time with you, too, Julian. Thank you for inviting me to come to Cuba. I think we get along amazingly well."

"And so I hope we'll have another wonderful day next Sunday."

"Definitely," I said. "I'm already looking forward to it." Which I was, because now the coming week without Julian was starting to feel hollow and a bit daunting.

The moon's silvery countenance was now sinking into the Atlantic. It was the perfect end of a perfectly memorable week in which I had seen and experienced so much: Old Havana, its main squares and graceful colonial buildings, music groups and dancing pensioners, cherished children in crisp, clean uniforms, the cemetery with its miracles and mysteries, recycled books, repurposed chocolate, affectionate people who were seemingly reluctant to show guests where they lived.

The day itself had been one of goodbyes: at the conference and at Muriel's place, where I took my leave of the ANGLO board and, from the corner of my eye, observed the villa's long goodbye to the good life before the revolution. And now, I suddenly realized, the hardest goodbye of all was going to be letting Julian go to the bus terminal to return to his family and life in Santa Clara.

"Well, have a good week," I said when he'd picked up his suitcase from Magdalena's. "And please say hello to your whole family for me."

"Thank you, Heather. I sincerely hope you will have a good week, too," he said, standing with his suitcase at the door. We hugged awkwardly and then he left.

8

LOOKING FOR COWBOYS IN VINALES

THE FOLLOWING MONDAY WAS MY first day of traveling alone in Cuba. As arranged the previous week, I was to take a tour to the western province of Pinar del Rio, center of Cuban tobacco-growing. The brochure had said the tour bus would leave at seven-thirty, so I left the still-quiet apartment just after seven, and tiptoed down the nine flights of narrow stairs with practiced ease.

The lobby of the high-rise Habana Libre hotel showed no sign of any activity, making me wonder whether the tour would leave on time. Gradually, however, sleepy tourists – mostly South American and Canadian couples – straggled in and slumped into the oversized armchairs.

I gazed around me at the considerable infrastructure of what had once been the Havana Hilton: several clothing boutiques, a coffee bar, a travel agent, a currency exchange. There was even an artificial Christmas tree for the tourists, sparsely hung with a few paper chains. With the summery weather, I'd almost forgotten that it would

92

soon be Christmas – but I'd be back in snowy Switzerland by then. Julian and I had come here the previous week to book my excursions at Cubatur, the state-run travel agency. At the time, I was astounded by the lack of advertising and the absence of customer information: there was only one tour brochure in the whole place, and it stayed on the agent's desk. After reading the single pamphlet, virtually cheek-to-cheek, Julian and I discussed my options.

"So, Heather, which tours will you take?"

"Well, Vinales looks very pretty and it also seems a good tour for one day. I think that might be a good one to start with, don't you? It's on Monday."

"Vinales, mhm, mhm. Yes, an excellent choice – very good. I was in Pinar del Rio many times in the sixties and seventies, inspecting English classes."

"And then, after that... I think maybe the two-day tour on Tuesday and Wednesday? The one to central Cuba? To Santa Clara and Trinidad and so on?"

"Uhuh, yes. But ehm did you see the price?" he asked, eyebrows raised.

"Yes, I did. OK, seventy CUCs is a lot, I know. But it's a good price for two days. Look, it includes an overnight stay in a motel; that's why it's more expensive." I didn't know exactly what he was thinking, but it occurred to me that my three days of travel were going to cost the equivalent of over four months of his salary. Anyway, that was that; I'd decided. Monday, Tuesday and Wednesday of my week alone would be spent on the road with Cubatur, and I'd spend the other three days sightseeing on my own in Havana.

While we were enjoying a celebratory juice in the coffee

bar, Julian told a good story about Fidel and the Habana Libre, murmuring it in my ear. During the first months post-revolution, Castro established his headquarters upstairs in the hotel, which was, at that time, still called the Havana Hilton. After a long day spent working for his people and country, Castro would regularly come down to the hotel bar for his favorite drink: a chocolate milkshake. Fidel's evening milkshake became so predictable that his enemies decided to make it a fatal flaw, and bribed the hotel barman to put poison in it. The poison had been smuggled into the bar and was ready for Fidel's next visit, when pro-Castro employees got wind of the plot. A raid on the hotel put an end to the barman's career, if not his life – and probably saved Castro's.

Now, here I was, back in the lobby of the Havana Libre, waiting patiently with other Cubatur customers to start the tour to Vinales. I was just debating whether to order a chocolate milkshake at the bar, when our guide came in to rouse us all from our armchair torpor and herd us onto the bus. His name was Vladimir and he was a tanned, broad-shouldered Cuban, who could have been mistaken for some kind of sports coach. Perhaps it was his athletic appearance that got him the job; it certainly wasn't his English. As soon as the bus started rolling, Vladimir provided a tour-guide commentary by reading off the names of streets, towns and villages and otherwise being minimally informative in both English and Spanish. His announcements finally petered out as we sped down the *Carretera Central* towards Pinar del Rio.

The non-existent commentary was no big loss, though, because what I could observe from the bus on this sunny, breezy day was fascinating. As there was almost no high-speed traffic on the highway, we shared the two lanes of the *carretera* with bicycles, battered trucks loaded with farm produce, horse-drawn carts, 1950s cars and truckload after truckload of standing passengers, holding on for dear life. Every once in a while there was a group of would-be travellers waiting on the side of the road, waving money at passing vehicles, hoping thus to catch a ride to the next town. As Julian had so often told me, transportation is one of Cuba's major problems. There are simply not enough buses and cars.

Farther back from the road, there were fields and small clusters of trees, both palm and deciduous. Many palms had obviously lost their tops in the recent hurricanes; probably many roofs had been blown off, too, but they were all back in place now, six weeks later. Some fields were being plowed or harrowed with implements straight out of a farming museum, dragged by teams of yoked oxen. There were virtually no tractors, and the few that I saw were on the road, pulling wagonloads of standing children, dressed in the national school uniform of a crisp white shirt, maroon shorts or skirt and a red or blue neck-scarf.

Farmers weren't the only ones trying to work without the help of machines. We passed several squads of highway maintenance men in straw hats, who were trying to cut back bushes on the center strip by whacking at them with dull *machetes*. A number of cowboys could also be seen: handsome young men in cowboy hats and high white boots, riding small but spirited horses along the edges of fields, often with a dog trotting behind. It seemed like the perfect lifestyle for this open landscape with small stands of trees and wide blue sky. Only the cattle were missing. Where were they?

After about an hour and a half of driving we reached the city of Pinar del Rio, which looked seriously run-down. The bus driver showed no intention of stopping, but just rumbled slowly through the center, bumping over the curbs as he turned the tight corners. There were a few dusty, gray public buildings and then countless low, partially painted, one– and two-story concrete houses, some with ornate, hand-carved wooden grills in the glassless windows.

Vladimir tapped on the microphone and cleared his throat. "This is Pinar del Rio, population hundred twenty thousand, capital of province Pinar del Rio. In order we have time visiting the *Cueva del Indio* before lunch we will not stop in Pinar. But I can tell you some things for this city... Pinar is home of *Fabrica de Tobaccos Donatien*, and they make very goods cigar. We gonna see cigar-making later – after Vinales – in da afternoon. And now we drive to Vinales." That was it. No one said a word. We had been lulled into a glassy-eyed trance by the long highway drive; the bus stumbled over a few more curbs as we left the provincial capital of 120,000 souls behind us, turning back towards the more picturesque town and valley of Vinales.

A short time later, we rolled to a stop at a place called Los Jazmines, a roadside look-off and hikers' hotel that affords a breathtaking view of the Vinales valley, which stretches northward into the distance. The long, pancake-flat valley made me think of the Garden of Eden, with clumps of palm trees, bright green fields and fantastic rock formations, called *mogotes,* all growing out of copper-red soil. Although I had already read about the *mogotes* of Vinales, they'd been difficult to imagine. They are straight-sided, flat-topped, stand-alone limestone mountains that appear to have popped up overnight like vine-draped mushrooms strewn over a vast, flat plain of red soil and green vegetation. There is something primordial about them; they make you think of the backdrop for a dinosaur movie. And when you contemplate the view down the whole valley, with isolated *mogotes* diminishing into the distance, you think of the topography of another planet.

We then drove into the valley, passing neat fields of tobacco plants, their leaves a vigorous green on top, silverish on the bottom. The local farmers and their families lived in pastel-painted bungalows that could not have consisted of more than two rooms. Some houses had palm-thatch roofs, while others were covered with corrugated metal. Nearly every house had a clothesline full of clean laundry flapping beside it, and hens and their chicks scratching for food in the yard.

The next stop was the town of Vinales itself, the most photogenic in the province. Attached blue and green bungalows now lined the main road that led uphill to the center of town. Many of them displayed signs in English or Spanish, advertising tourist rooms, often with a family member posted on the veranda in case any tourists happened by. Then came the row of shops, looking like scenery for a cowboy movie, with columned arcades providing sidewalk shade. Vladimir pointed out a bakery, a butcher's shop, a post office, an ice cream kiosk – all minute, all open for business. And there were plenty of shoppers: men in straw cowboy hats and jeans, and women in full, crinolined skirts, carrying parasols to keep the sun off their faces. It was like stepping back in time to the American Wild West – except for the young people, who showed a preference for spandex-and-jeans or satin basketball uniforms.

"OK, we have a forty minutes stop in Vinales. Forty minutes!" Vladimir barked before releasing us into the Wild West of Cuba. I jumped down onto the raised wooden sidewalk and walked back down the street, taking pictures of yesteryear. I joined the crowd in front of one small shop to find out what people were buying. It was bread. This was placed in cloth bags passed over the counter along with the ration booklet that Cubans call *la libreta*. The family's bread was put directly into the bag, without wrapping, and the date and amount recorded in the *libreta*. Magdalena had shown me her *libreta* the previous day. It entitled her to buy subsidized items, like milk, eggs, flour, beans and sugar at a very low price, or in some cases to get them free. As I was strolling along the raised sidewalk, taking pictures of cowboys and vintage cars, a group of Canadian cyclists rode past, dressed in state-of-the-art biking gear. It looked like fun and seemed like a wonderful way to spend a holiday, especially in view of the weather and sparse traffic.

After Vinales came the previously announced *Cueva del Indio*, which Vladimir regarded as one of the two highlights of the tour.

"Now you gonna see something very especial: a big cave with a river in it," he announced.

After a steep climb up a rocky path, we entered the cave, which we stumbled through in the dim light, eventually coming to an underground river in which motorboats were waiting. Each driver filled his boat with a dozen tourists, then started downriver towards the mouth of the cave, pointing out imagined objects in the limestone formations as we passed by. For those who like caves, it was spectacular.

Vladimir next invited us to a "Cuban ranch" for a late lunch. It was actually a rustic outdoor restaurant, where trestle tables had been set up under palm-leaf roofing, The ambient air by this time was lovely: warm enough for short sleeves; breezy, but not humid. Seated on both sides of two big tables, we bus passengers relaxed and started chatting. We were served "traditional Cuban dishes": roast pork, long beans, yucca, fried plantains, rice and black beans (called *moros y cristianos* or "Moors and Christians"). Ten musicians and a female singer entertained us throughout the meal. They sounded authentic and made the whole occasion feel fun and carefree, especially because they smiled and interacted with each other while playing. It occurred to me that they were the first Afro-Cubans we'd encountered that day. I had noticed none among the farmers, highway workers, cowboys, motorboat drivers, restaurant servers or inhabitants of Vinales. Julian had mentioned that Cubans were darker toward the eastern end of Cuba, and we were in the west.

Conversation during the meal was relaxed but impersonal. People mostly chatted about their good and bad experiences with hotels, restaurants and night clubs. I didn't have much to contribute, seeing as I was staying at Magdalena's. Then one of the Canadian women came back from the washroom and giggled to her husband:

"Hey, know what? There's a sign in the washroom that says not to put the toilet paper in the toilet. Where the heck are you supposed to put it?"

"In the waste paper basket next to the toilet," I said, breaking the embarrassed silence.

"Oh my God!" she said, "I've been flushing the paper all the time."

A man next to her husband spoke up: "I think it's OK in the big hotels, but in smaller places it's not. I'm a plumber, so I pay attention to that sort of thing. It's because they don't really have enough water pressure here, so they have to, like, create pressure by using narrow pipes. That means you can't flush even toilet tissue, or else it might block the whole system…. It's the same all over South America – and in southern Europe, too, for that matter."

There was more silence and a few nervous chuckles as other group members digested the new information. Just then, we were all distracted by the sight of two cowboys on horseback, racing each other just for the hell of it. They galloped the length of the next field to the loud cheering of all guests, pulling up short just as they came to the ditch at the end.

When I noticed the cowboys dismounting, I left the table, thinking I might be able to talk to them or at least take their picture. Like the other cowboys I'd seen earlier, riding beside the highway or walking the main street of Vinales, these two men were wearing large, full-brimmed straw hats, khaki shirts, blue jeans and knee-high white rubber boots. They were probably in their thirties, slight but muscular, tanned and healthy.

"*Hola*" I said, smiling broadly. "*Tengo una pregunta.*" (I have a question.)

"*Buenos dias, senora.*" They waited for my question, squinting against the sun.

"Where are your cows?" I managed to ask in Spanish. It was an innocent question – I was just wondering where they kept them.

"*Vacas*? We don't have cows," laughed one, "we're tobacco farmers."

"But… but you have horses…. Why not cows?" I stuttered, surprised.

"Yes, we have horses for going to the fields," they explained. "We have no tractor, no truck."

"*Ah, vale*," I said. "Right, you have no tractor…" Then, wracking my brain for another question, I asked: "*Te gusta la vida de cultivador*?" (Do you like the life of a farmer?)

"*Si si*," they assured me emphatically, "*como no*?" And why wouldn't they like a life outdoors in the saddle in such pleasant weather?

"Now, listen please." It was Vladimir again. "I gonna show you how we make Cuban cigars. OK, first we look on a tobacco plant. Here… You see this one here? Is tall – taller than me. And has diffren' leafs. Top leaf, bottom leaf, middle leaf. And they have diffren' taste: top leafs are strong, lotta sun – you see the small leafs up here? – but bottom leafs down here – big one – are mild, yeah?"

A half-hour after lunch we were on a tobacco farm,

learning about what goes into a good cigar. Vladimir was obviously much happier doing this part of the tour. We next walked into a curing shed or drying barn, a large building where stacks of tobacco leaves were hung from the rafters to dry. Vladimir again explained a number of curing distinctions, but most of us just basked in the building's twilight, glad to be momentarily out of the sun and inhaling the fragrant air. The tobacco farmer, dressed in a loose white pajama-suit topped with a wide-brimmed straw hat, went around with our group. He seemed uncomfortable to be the object of our attention, yet proud of his tobacco and buildings. He spoke no English, but exchanged a few words of Spanish with Vladimir from time to time.

Outside the curing barn a wiry old man, his walnut-colored skin deeply wrinkled, sat at an old wooden desk, waiting to do his cigar-rolling demonstration. He said not a word, but showed us with exaggerated gestures how to create a cigar by combining the three different kinds of tobacco leaf, expertly rolling them into a tight and even cylinder, and finally slicing off both ends with a rounded tobacco knife, his manual dexterity obviously acquired through long practice.

As we walked back to the bus I noticed a group of five painted stones in the front yard of the farmer's bungalow. The stones – each about six inches across – were painted to look like heads with faces; there was a different name written below each face. I asked Vladimir what it was all about.

"Oh, is a long story," he discouraged me, obviously not wanting to get too involved in telling it. "Dey are da

Miami Five. You know it?" I said I'd never heard of the Miami Five.

"Men in prison – in USA," he said by way of explanation and moved on quickly to chat with another tourist. I was left to figure out the rest for myself. I would have to ask Julian when I saw him again.

Finally, after a visiting a cigar store offering "special discounts", we boarded the bus for the drive back to Havana. I closed my eyes and meditated on Cuban daily life and the different realities we'd experienced in the course of the day. First of all there was the hard reality of traveling anywhere else in Cuba, of flagging down a truck, or of standing and holding on tight in your tractor-drawn "school bus". Then there was the reality of dealing with tourists who are rich enough to spend eight months' Cuban salary on a box of cigars without batting an eye, yet seem totally ignorant of how toilets work and persist in flushing toilet paper, when everyone knows that this will clog the pipes. There were also the amazing discrepancies in Cuban performance, with lots of know-how and even top-level expertise in tobacco-growing and cigar-making, hurricane-predicting and life-saving, medical research and treatment, yet with low-tech equipment from the nineteenth century in plumbing and plowing, distribution and transport.

———— •••• ————

Vladimir and his driver got us back to Havana a little after 7 p.m., so I went straight home. Magdalena was there, of course, and had saved me a plate of fried *boniato* chips – Cuban sweet potato – as a snack. I sat down in the living room to eat it and watch TV with her. It was news time and we were shown Fidel's brother, Raul Castro, woodenly reading a speech at a meeting of South American leaders in Brazil, the front of his dark business suit decorated with a sash in Cuba's colors of red, white and blue. He was talking about Cuba's efforts towards economic integration with Latin America.

"*No es verdad*! It's not true at all," she muttered, shaking her head in amazement at his audacity.

"But he's more realistic than his brother, no? He wants Cubans to have their own business and earn more money."

"Ha! They say you can have a business and then make it impossible with regulations. For example, the *casas particulares*. It's possible to have paying guests in your home, but then the rules are so complicated and the license is so expensive, that it's better to do nothing. That's the reality in Cuba. *Si, si, senor Castro*!"

As I continued to watch Raul delivering his speech I wondered what his reality was. Did he have a *libreta*? Could he buy whatever he wanted? How much was he affected by Cuba's shortages of transport and water, food and electricity?

9
FINDING CHE IN SANTA CLARA

A FTER PACKING A SMALL OVERNIGHT bag on Monday evening, I returned to Magdalena's living room to remind her that I'd be away for two days. By this time she was watching a Venezuelan soap opera.

"Magdalena," I began, "I forgot to tell you – I'm going on a tour of central Cuba for two days. That means I won't be here tomorrow night."

"Tomorrow? You're not here? Because you're visiting Julian?"

"No, no. I'm going on a tour, with Cubatur."

"*Ah, si si si.* On a bus. Good. Where are you going?"

"To Santa Clara and, and Trinidad and Cienfuegos and…"

"*Bueno.* Trinidad is beautiful, very beautiful. But be very careful!"

Thereupon followed a demonstration of how to clasp a handbag to one's bosom with both hands, and how to turn one's back to the street when accessing one's change-purse. According to Magdalena, Cuba was full of criminals.

<hr>

When I got to the Habana Libre at seven the following morning, it was much livelier than the previous day. Several tour buses already lined the street, their drivers chatting and smoking on the curb while their motors spewed black exhaust into the morning freshness. I had just settled into one of the hotel's plump armchairs, when a trim woman in a yellow Cubatur polo-shirt and navy slacks came jogging through the revolving door to announce my tour. Yesterday we had started nearly an hour later than the advertised departure time; today it was going to be a little earlier. I would just have to get used to the flexibility of timetables here.

Our guide's name was Berta, an energetic peroxide-blond in her late forties. She announced – in very good English – that she was going to do the tour in English and Spanish. That was fine with everyone on the bus, because a number of us were less than fluent in Spanish. Among my fellow passengers, I can recall two Korean dentistry students, a man and two young women from London, who were in Havana for the film festival, three single men from Belgium and Switzerland, and a young honeymoon couple from Mexico.

<hr>

Berta stood in the aisle, addressing us via microphone as we barreled down the A1 out of Havana towards the province of Matanzas. The tour, she announced, would take us to Santa Clara and Sancti Spiritus today, Trinidad and Cienfuegos tomorrow. But first, after about an hour of driving, we would stop at what she called a "tourist trap", because they had clean toilets and safe drinks, and we could walk around, stretch our legs and look at some Cuban animals for free. As Berta was announcing this, we passed a group of people waiting on the side of the road. In front of them, clipboard in hand, stood a woman in a yellow overall, flagging down cars.

"Oh, yeah," Berta commented, "what you can see here is some peoples waiting for a drive to the next town – or maybe further – in a car or truck. The woman in yellow is an *amarilla*, a yellow traffic officer, what means that she can stop the cars with not enough passengers and make them to pick up the peoples waiting here. You know we have a few problems in Cuba, and transportation is one of these. There are not enough buses. So this is one thing we have to do. You will also see some school buses and small trucks from Canada on the road. They were a present to the Cuban people from Canada. That is because Canada has a program – they give us their old trucks and buses. So thank you, Canada!" Her thanks made me proud of my Canadian passport.

Berta went on to tell us other things about Cuba, blemishes and all. She was frank and critical, but usually positive. She told us quite a bit about herself, too: that she earned 400 Cuban pesos a month – about $16 – and that she worked four days a week on average. This was enough to enable her to live in a subsidized two-room apartment with her mother and daughter and to buy food for them all. Of course her mother received a pension, and her daughter worked as well. Berta was "quite happy" with her job, she said. By way of comparison she reported that a Cuban medical doctor earned $24 a month, and that Cuba produced thousands of doctors a year, exporting some of them to other countries like Venezuela, Ecuador and Angola. Cuban medical care was excellent and free, she said, including cosmetic surgery. At this, a loud murmur arose from the London camp, one of whom then shouted, "Have you tried it?"

"Yes," replied Berta with a wink, "three times!"

Berta's "tourist trap" with its collection of animals had sounded rather attractive, and it was. Miscellaneous Cuban species, like large lizards, small deer, crocodiles and tiny jewel-colored tropical birds were on display. It was where I met my first *jutias*, a sort of possum-like tree-rat that Cubans hunted to virtual extinction during the so-called "special period" in the 1990s, when there was almost no other meat available.

The "tourist trap" fulfilled its promise in every way, but after twenty minutes we were ready to straggle back to the bus and continue on to Santa Clara, where the *Memorial al Che* awaited us. Located in a grassy park on the outskirts of the city, the memorial was designed to impress. It is constructed of monumental slabs of concrete and marble, which, like so many buildings in Cuba, are in a state of dilapidation. The enormous bronze statue of Che Guevara atop the monument shows him looking energetic and tough, one arm in a plaster cast and the other holding up a rifle. A loudspeaker blares a patriotic song that is unfortunately rendered incomprehensible by its high volume. A nearby billboard reads: *Queremos que sean como el Che – Fidel* (We want you to be like Che. – Fidel). During the day, buses from all over the country pull up and disgorge classes of school children, who have come to visit the shrine of their national hero.

The memorial's interior houses a museum and a mausoleum, the latter holding the mortal remains of Ernesto "Che" Guevara and thirty of his comrades killed in the Bolivian campaign of 1967, which have been repatriated over the last twenty years and buried with full honors. Designed as a dark, low-ceilinged grotto with a flickering eternal flame, the mausoleum exudes an atmosphere of subdued grief and religious devotion. Even school children are silent in the presence of Che's spirit.

After paying our respects in the grotto, our group visited the Che Museum along with a large group of well-behaved school children of eight or nine years, who were clearly excited to be there. Lined up in hand-holding pairs, they followed their teacher through the exhibits and listened attentively to her explanations. The most interesting displays were of Che's uniforms and weapons, and of early photographs of Guevara and Castro and their co-revolutionaries during training for their invasion of Cuba, during their time as *guerrilleros* in the Sierra Maestra mountains, and during their triumphal entry into Havana. The photos are touching reminders of the youth and idealism of the revolution's early days, but I was surprised that the children were so interested in these fifty-year-old artifacts. When we emerged from the museum, the same melody as before greeted us from the monument's loudspeakers. It was a song addressed to "Commandante Che Guevara" and the children, who knew it by heart, sang along.

At lunch I sat with the two Korean dental students, who were studying at the University of Missouri. They were spending their long Christmas vacation in Cuba and Mexico. Despite their exposure to English in lectures and labs at their university, they complained that they couldn't understand a word Berta said, and had therefore had trouble not only with facts about Cuba, but also with her instructions. There was no danger that this would ruin the trip for them, however, as they were determined to see, taste, touch and do as much as they possibly could to experience Cuba first-hand. This they demonstrated by trying every single item offered by the extensive lunch buffet, including four or five different desserts.

Our next sight-seeing stop in Santa Clara was the site of the heroic and most decisive battle of the revolution, in which Che and a small group of men used a bulldozer to tear up the railway tracks and thus derail a strategic pro-Batista train that was carrying guns, ammunition and over 400 government troops. The train is still there, spilled and sprawled all over the tracks with the bulldozer smugly looking on. Berta painted a dramatic picture of Che and his band of eighteen men surrounding the derailed train in the dark, and threatening the bewildered commanding officer with instant death if he refused to surrender.

As we listened to her account, I couldn't help hearing the clip-clop of horses on the road behind us. Out of the corner of my eye I discerned a covered horse-drawn wagon passing at a trot, with two benches for passengers along the sides of the wagon. I did a double take. Was there some kind of Mennonite group in Santa Clara? No, the people in the wagon were typical Cubans: women wearing sleeveless tops in bright colors and men in baseball caps and polo-shirts. Another wooden wagon rattled past as I fumbled my camera out of my backpack. Then it hit me: they were horse-drawn trams transporting people from one side of Santa Clara to the other. Another solution to the transport problem. I wondered if Julian or his wife ever took these trams. And then I thought about Julian a little more and wondered if I might run into to him while in Santa Clara. It was unlikely, given that his medical school was not in the center of town, and particularly since neither of us had a cell phone.

Santa Clara seemed decades behind Havana in terms of technology. The traffic was tamer, the pace was slower. I saw dump-trucks driving through the center with about twenty passengers – mostly men – standing in the back, holding on tight and looking over the rim. Mothers, accompanying their children on the way home from school, stood in the street and chatted with acquaintances. There were department stores on the main streets that consisted of an open front and a large counter, where customers requested items while standing on the sidewalk and sales clerks disappeared into the interior to fetch them.

Even though Santa Clara has a population of nearly a quarter million, it seems like a smaller town because it has a green and quiet center – the Parque Vidal. This is a large, tree-lined plaza filled with toddlers chasing pigeons, resting shoppers, men in twos and threes discussing baseball, romantic couples entwined in each other's arms, grandmothers resting... all very innocent, all very old-fashioned. According to Berta, something like the Italian *passeggiata* takes place there every evening: citizens of all ages come to the Parque Vidal to stroll, see and be seen. Around the square are magnificent and beautifully restored colonial or neo-colonial buildings, most notably the José Marti library, the Teatro La Caridad, and the Museo de Artes Decorativas. The central historical figure in Santa Clara is Marta Abreu, a wealthy heiress who donated schools, laundries, her own home and a theater to the town. The Teatro la Caridad (or Charity Theatre) is so named because its proceeds were designated for schools for the poor.

Although I walked round the whole Parque Vidal, hoping to run into Julian, I failed to spot him. The only person I talked to was a friendly man who could speak excellent German; he asked me for 10 CUCs at the end of our conversation. It was now time to leave Santa Clara and move on south-eastwards to Sancti Spiritus. Berta had given us forty-five minutes to explore Santa Clara on our own, so the Cubatur bus would be waiting just off the main square. One of the last things she'd warned us about before letting us loose was "eating street food". This was because she didn't want any toilet emergencies on the drive to Sancti Spiritus. As we all drifted back to the bus from various street corners, I spied the two Koreans strolling along the opposite sidewalk, each holding a cone of bright yellow ice-cream.

"Oh no," I thought to myself, "what flavor did they

get? Ptomaine or salmonella?" When she saw them, Berta rolled her eyes and turned to me.

"Heather, they are sitting behind you in the bus, no? Could you please, please make sure they understand me?" she pleaded. I agreed to act as an interpreter from then on.

We still had to wait for the Mexican honeymoon couple, who could usually be spotted from a distance because they were eternally wrapped in each other's embrace. She was doll-like and spoke with the soft, high voice of a twelve-year-old; he was rotund and moved with all the authority of his new status as a married man. On the bus or off, they remained engrossed in each other, not paying much attention to the rest of us.

———•••———

Sancti Spiritus is not nearly as big as Santa Clara but seems much older, dating from the early 1500s. We wandered as a group around the oldest part, with its narrow cobblestone streets and a somewhat bedraggled cathedral. Finally, we came to rest next to a gracefully arched, humpback bridge, the Puente Yayabo, which we gazed at appreciatively as we drank our Cuban *Cristal* beers on a terrace overlooking the river.

Day One of the tour was moving towards its end. The Korean students had, disappointingly, failed to show any signs of discomfort after their ice cream. In fact, instead of sitting with the rest of our group on the terrace, they opted to join local youth in a game of street stickball, played with a broom handle and an egg-sized stone. The Koreans adored baseball, and it was obvious that this was the highlight of their day so far. They took photos of each other up at bat and were allowed hits by their gracious Cuban hosts, all without using more than a few words of English. Their luck continued when we arrived at *Los Laureles*, our accommodation for the night, and found a whole Cuban baseball team in the lobby, suited up and waiting to be taken to the local stadium. Their baseball uniforms were bright turquoise, and the Koreans wasted no time in borrowing the shirts straight off two players' backs so that they could take pictures of each other, posing – complete with bats and hats – as Cuban baseball stars.

Once again, Berta gave us a speech about being careful with water and uncooked food. "And don't drink the free juice here!" she said, "It's just made with powder and the local water." Then she looked pointedly at me and motioned towards the Koreans. By now, whenever Berta announced anything, the Koreans automatically came to my side for a simplified version; they were not trying to be difficult.

At suppertime in the *Los Laureles* restaurant, I sat with Berta, who was eating alone. She actually seemed happy to have company, so I didn't feel bad about seizing the opportunity to ask a bit more about herself and her country.

"When I was 22, I got scholarship to Bulgaria to study touristic," she said. "That was in the 1980s."

I made a horrified face. "No, no. It wasn't so bad," she said.

"Isn't Bulgaria a pretty dull country?"

"Not really," she said, "we had a good touristic course

and I learned French there. And that was where I met my ex-husband. Yes, he was Bulgarian, but when he came back to Cuba with me, he suddenly got a special interest in Cuban dancers. Hah, yes! So that was the end of our marriage. In those days we learned Russian at school in Cuba, so I picked up Bulgarian pretty quick."

So if her daughter was half Bulgarian, I wanted to know, did she want to go off and live somewhere outside Cuba?

No, said Berta, she had a good job as a receptionist in a big hotel in Havana and liked her job a lot. It also meant she earned CUCs instead of pesos and that helped the family cover its expenses.

It occurred to me that Berta must also earn quite a few CUCs per week in tips, and that such earnings would be worth more than her salary. Maybe her claim of living well on sixteen CUCs a month had to be taken with a large grain of salt.

As we were talking, a muscular young man with big hair, dressed in nothing but wrinkled khaki shorts came up to our table. He was part of a theater troupe rehearsing at *Los Laureles*, he said, and asked if we'd like to be part of a trial audience for their play, which they were dress-rehearsing that evening. I said I would come along, despite my bad Spanish, but Berta said she had to go to bed early.

At seven-thirty, when the play was supposed to start, I returned to the motel restaurant and met up with the two Swiss men and the two female movie fans from London. The five of us were then led to the back of the motel complex, where there was a small stage in an open courtyard. The audience sat on folding chairs in this theater under the stars.

We were told that the troupe consisted of four actors – two women, two men – plus a crew of two: a girl who did make-up and costume changes and a young man who changed scenery and handled lighting. They were all in their twenties. They had written the play themselves, which was about a young Cuban who – surprise, surprise – lived in a mountain village in eastern Cuba. I was worried that my Spanish might fail me completely, but it turned out that I could understand far more than half of what was said.

The plot was rather simple: Manuel has just finished high school. One day, his former teacher visits and leaves information about a training scheme for young volunteers to serve in medical aid programs. Manuel is clearly interested in volunteering, but the situation at home makes this difficult: his mother needs his earnings and she is ill with some unnamed disease – probably cancer. Manuel tells his friend Carlos about the training scheme while they are working in the forest. Carlos is not impressed; he says Manuel should get a girlfriend rather than help people on the other side of the world. Manuel admits that he has his eye on Roxana, a girl from the same village. There follows a comic scene in which Carlos, playing Roxana, tries to teach Manuel to dance.

At this point, I was expecting a happy end in which Manuel would marry the girl and then maybe get medical training and cure his mother. But things didn't turn out like that. First of all, Carlos – not Manuel – charms Roxana into going to a dance with him. And second, instead of fighting for Roxana, Manuel decides that serving the common good is more important than staying in the village with the two women he loves. There is only a glimmer of hope for a happy end: when he announces his decision to leave for paramedical training, his mother and Roxana are clearly impressed by his strength of character.

I – and probably the rest of the trial audience – felt somewhat disappointed with the outcome, but we clapped politely and thanked the actors for inviting us. They were not so easily satisfied, however: they wanted to hear what we actually thought of the play, and where it could be improved. This was when one of the young women from London suggested that the audience should discuss its reactions briefly in English and then she and her friend would translate our feedback into Spanish. The two women were Linda from Spain and Carolina from Colombia. Both were graceful and beautiful, with long dark hair. They worked as cultural attachés for their countries in London, and as bilingual speakers were in a perfect position to collect and pass on our feedback.

We discussed the play in English for about twenty minutes, while the troupe dismantled props and lighting. Our general feeling was that the acting was natural, but that the plot took a sudden and unexpected turn with Manuel's decision at the end; we wanted a "more human" ending and more humor, like the learning-to-dance scene. And wouldn't it be more interesting, we suggested, if Manuel wasn't so high-minded? The actors were shocked. Manuel represents Che Guevara's "new man", they said. He is prepared to act on his principles and live or die for the common good, rather than for his own personal

117

happiness. Without new men, socialism would only be possible in a dictatorship, they argued. People had to learn to change their goals and motivation, otherwise we'd be stuck in the same old self-interest as always. They had a point. But we just shook our heads at the actors' idealism, feeling cynical and decadent. Carolina from Colombia, who was well versed in political theory, argued with them for a long time, but the rest of us begged off and returned to our rooms. Socialist theory – even if it came from Che himself – felt abstract and boring. I had definitely become more cynical about politics in the forty-plus years since my Socialist-Worker days in New York. To achieve any kind of fair distribution of land, resources and happiness, it was true that people would have to become a whole lot less partial to their own family, region and race. But I didn't know if the majority would ever choose to become more altruistic.

As I got ready for bed, I reflected on Che's continuing importance in Cuban life. He's a national idol, a Christ-like martyr who suffered and died for the poor and oppressed, a modern philosopher, a role-model for all Cubans, a superman. School children pledge allegiance to him every morning. Songs, like prayers, are addressed to him. His picture appears on a thousand more walls than Fidel Castro's. Now immortal and incorruptible, he's more valuable to the revolution dead than alive.

10
CENTRAL CUBA: TRINIDAD AND CIENFUEGOS

MY ROOM IN THE *Los Laureles* motel was large and clean, but windowless. To make up for the lack of view, it had air-conditioning and a jumbo flat-screen satellite TV that allowed me to watch CNN any time I wanted. Like the internet, uncensored satellite TV appeared to be available for tourists but not for Cubans. Regrettably, I felt little motivation to catch up with news from the outside world; I was too excited about finally seeing Trinidad, which both Julian and Magdalena had said was the most beautiful town in Cuba.

Breakfast at *Los Laureles* was better than supper, and even featured a cook standing ready to take orders at an omelet station, just like in posh hotels. Most of us were up and in the dining room by seven, as prescribed by Berta, so that the day's tour could start at eight. As we entered, she stood at the door, reminding us that the juice ban was still in effect:

"Remember, please do not, do NOT, drink the juice

for breakfast. It's like to drink the normal water, right? And do not forget to buy your bottle drink for the day."

The Mexican newly-weds were not at breakfast, and still hadn't appeared by the time the rest of us boarded the bus. There was a wait of ten minutes while Berta fumed in the front seat, sharing her anger with the driver. Finally she stomped back to the motel, pounded on the couple's door and entered. A minute later, all three of them were moving towards the bus: Berta marching in front, her countenance grim, while the Mexicans stumbled along behind, bleary-eyed, disheveled, but still hand-in-hand, dragging their massive honeymoon suitcase. They were greeted with weak grins and strained silence.

From the outskirts of Sancti Spiritus we drove south down a pretty valley; the Escambray Mountains, which looked perfect for hiking, rose on our right. The valley floor was covered by pastures with – incongruously to my eyes – sparse palm trees growing in them. Berta pointed out the different kinds of palms: the Cuban royal palm, very straight and tall and fast-growing, bottle palms of various wine-bottle shapes – also tall – and finally, belly palms, which looked pregnant with a bulge in the middle of their trunk.

Everything was green. Just as I was mentally trying to name the different shades of green I could distinguish – Kelly-green sugar cane, blue-green rushes, dark-emerald palm fronds, yellow-green grass – the bus turned off onto a side track lined with small shacks that teemed with children and chickens. We were headed towards what looked like a mansion. This turned out to be the Manaca-Iznaga estate, a former sugar plantation and *ingenio,* or sugar mill, that had belonged to one of the area's leading colonial families. Hundreds of slaves would have worked on this plantation in the 18th and 19th centuries, planting and cutting sugar cane, pressing the juice from the cane with an ox-powered press, and boiling it down into sugar for export. A short distance from the extensive plantation mansion there was a pagoda-like tower forty-five meters high, each of its seven stories smaller than the one below it. In the plantation's heyday, a huge bell – now lying in the grass in front of the mansion – was hung at the top of the tower and rung to signal the beginning and end of daily fieldwork, as well as emergencies, such as fires or escaping slaves.

Visitors are permitted to walk up the tower's inner wooden stairs and look through the openings on each of the seven levels, which many of us did. The Korean students swarmed over the tower, taking photos of each other hanging out from the railings at alarming lengths and angles. From the top, it seemed likely that the shacks we had driven past on our way up to the mansion were the remnants of slave housing from bygone days. Carolina looked down at the tiny front yards with their jumble of old farm implements, broken furniture and chickens.

"It doesn't look like much has changed down there in 250 years," she remarked.

"Yeah, but the black peoples in Cuba now have jobs and social security, just like white people," replied our guide. "Believe me, they don't have to live like that."

"Well, the ones down there in those little houses don't

seem to get much help from the government," remarked Carolina. Berta raised her eyebrows, shrugged her hands and rolled her eyes, but would say no more. She was keeping her thoughts to herself.

By the time I got to the bottom of the tower again, my Korean wards had already torn off to explore the mansion. At first glance there is nothing much to explore; the mansion has become a modern tourist restaurant, full of cafeteria-style tables and gliding waiters. The Koreans had, however, skipped right through the mansion and out the other side, climbing down into a large pit housing a cane press that was once driven by an ox, or a pair of oxen, walking around in circles. They were now playing oxen and, by pushing the wooden arms of the press, were managing to turn the huge stone wheel, thus crushing a few stalks of sugar cane scavenged from a source I did not want to contemplate. A small amount of *guarapo* trickled into a pan at the bottom of the press. "You take video, yes?" one of them grunted, handing me his camera. I was only too glad to oblige. They were having a great time in the adventure park they kept trying to conjure out of Cuba.

Our next stop was Trinidad itself, and it was obvious why we'd come here as soon as we got off our bus near the Plaza Mayor or main square. The park has an Alice-in-Wonderland charm, offering a stylized landscape of topiary trees, classical statues, large porcelain vases set upon pedestals, and single royal palms providing dappled shade for wrought-iron benches. It is highly photogenic, yet formal in a way one rarely associates with Cuba. A couple of interesting characters were sitting around on the benches: a dapper, velvet-suited 19th century gentleman smoking a huge cigar, and a colorful colonial lady complete with long dress, parasol and hanging silk purse. As soon as my fellow tourists had whipped out their cameras, the characters came to life and requested money – a dollar, in fact – for having their picture taken. Blatant commercialism clashed with the surreal, frozen-in-time atmosphere of the square: the cameras were re-pocketed immediately. It's funny how we want to catch the natural beauty, the special character, the picturesqueness of a people and country as long as they remain unaware of their picturesqueness. We are digital hunters and gatherers, capturing innocence and grace and authenticity, which we frame with our imaginations to bring home and say, "Look what I shot while I was hunting for beauty in Cuba." But as soon as our prey turn to us and want money for posing, the act of photography loses its wild one-sidedness and turns into a commercial transaction that ruins the fun of the hunt.

The next item on Berta's agenda was a mansion full of colonial furniture called the Museo Romantico. The museum, which faces directly onto the main square, is situated in the 200-year-old house of the Brunets, one of the wealthy land-owning families of this sugar-producing region. It illustrates all aspects of colonial domestic life, from ornate sitting rooms to bathrooms. Once again, our Korean dentists-to-be outdid themselves in finding unusual venues for selfies as well as for photos of each other. There is little security – electronic or otherwise – in Cuban museums, which meant that the Koreans amused themselves by posing on centuries-old furniture and porcelain toilets.

———••·•———

The hilly cobblestone streets of Trinidad were lined with hundreds of beautifully restored pastel houses in the colonial bungalow style. Their roofs, covered in interlocking red clay tiles, added to the harmonious impression. I was fully satisfied with my photographic booty by the time we reached Trinidad's Casa de la Trova for a cold drink and an introduction to Cuban music and dance. A live band of about ten elderly musicians, straight out of the Buenavista Social Club, played and played, accompanied by a pair of young dancers whose job it was to demonstrate Cuban dances and then animate tourists to dance with them. Berta was already up on her feet and dancing casually with the bandleader, who resembled a scrawny Louis Armstrong. The two professional dancers, dressed in skin-tight Lycra, demonstrated an athletic salsa with carefully choreographed moves. Then the male dancer asked our Carolina to dance, while his female counterpart tried her luck with one of the Swiss men. As a Columbian, Carolina had no trouble looking good on the dance floor, but I sweated with dread as the professionals relentlessly worked their way through our group until it was my turn. By some miracle the male dancer had me moving to the rhythm – and maybe even looking like I knew what I was doing – within about two minutes. Mission accomplished, he moved on to his next victim, leaving me in the custody of a Swiss tour-mate. The band played on until Berta decided it was time to go. Strangely enough, the Koreans had disappeared during the dancing; for once, they were too shy to interact with Cubans.

From the Casa de la Trova we proceeded to our lunch restaurant of the day, located in a very quiet cobblestone street at the top of town. Here, too, live music greeted us as we straggled through the door. This time it was a *son* group called RaZon, consisting of two men on guitars and a young woman, who played bongos and flute and did most of the complex harmonizing. I bought one of their CDs during the meal. They were absolutely brilliant, and by this time everyone in our group was into Cuban music, swaying in their chairs as they ate, even humming along with the song from the Che Guevara Memorial, which was one of Razon's favorite numbers. The tune is extremely catchy, although the words about "the clear, endearing transparency of your beloved presence, Commander Che Guevara" lose quite a bit in translation.

Enjoying music together opened us up to each other too, so that, as we walked back from Trinidad's ancient center to rejoin our bus, we started linking arms and humming, or even dancing a few steps and taking pictures – pictures of each other, of ordinary Cubans embroidering tablecloths while seated in their doorways, of a father pushing his heavily laden bike with his small son on the crossbar, of fifty-year-old cars, of pastel houses with hand-carved wooden grills over their glassless windows.

It was here, too, that I finally solved the mystery of the Miami Five. In Santa Clara and Trinidad we'd noticed recurrent graffiti urging "freedom for our five brothers" (*Libertad para nuestros 5 hermanos*). Two days earlier, Vladimir had evaded my question about the Miami Five by saying it was a long story, but when we pointed out a stencil-sprayed wall slogan, Berta was more forthcoming:

"Yes, it's a famous group of five Cubans who been in jail in Miami USA for years and years. The North Americans say that they are spies – you know, espying for Cuba – but it's not true. So all Cubans want that they are free again and can return home." We accepted this explanation without comment, but in private had to wonder what the five "famous" Cubans had been doing in the US in the first place. They couldn't have been refugees or migrants if Castro was so keen on getting them back.

When we reached the bus we were all present except for the Mexicans. This time Berta was not upset at all, but wore a sweet, satisfied smile. She announced that the Mexicans had chosen to spend the rest of their honeymoon in a Trinidad *casa particular*, and had abandoned us without so much as an *adios*, merely informing her that they had now reached their final destination. Actually, with regular bus transport being so limited and crowded in Cuba, guidebooks often recommend that foreign travelers book a tour and then leave it in order to reach a specific destination fast and in comfort. And that is apparently what the Mexicans had done.

From Trinidad, our bus followed the Caribbean coast towards Cienfuegos. I kept telling myself, "Wow, this is the Caribbean," and looking at the color of the water. In fact, it didn't look too different from any other calm, light-blue water. The only other things I observed were several small fishing boats slowly making their way towards the open sea, a few narrow beaches and a healthy supply of flotsam and jetsam floating in the inlets.

Our last stop on the tour was the city of Cienfuegos, a relatively modern Cuban city founded by French settlers in 1819. It had broader streets and more space between the buildings than other cities I'd so far seen. We were allowed forty-five minutes on our own in downtown Cienfuegos, where we were dropped off in the Parque José Marti. I reduced this to thirty-five minutes when I repeated Berta's instructions to the two Koreans. The spacious park itself was treeless and swept clean of anything other than a larger-than-life statue of national hero José Marti at its far end, standing on a pedestal and exhorting us all to value freedom, with an appropriately large Cuban flag furling and unfurling behind him. Across the street, at my end of the square, was a huge billboard topped by a picture of Che Guevara, which said: TU EJEMPLO VIVE, TUS IDEAS PERDURAN. As with the song, the billboard slogan, "Your example lives, your ideas will endure", was addressed not to the people but to Che himself, as if he were some sort of holy figure who was omnipresent and therefore could be addressed in death. It reminded me of the words on religious shrines.

The clean-swept feeling of the main square extended to the streets around it. I walked up a pedestrian shopping-street wide enough to have little sales-stands running down the middle. They were selling jewelry and woodcarvings, mineral water, fast food, scarves and hats. Desperate to buy a few souvenirs to take home, I chose two pairs of dangly silver earrings for my sister and myself, and two Che berets for Swiss friends. Everything was amazingly cheap, but, still, priced in CUCs. The sellers looked like students, but may just have been young people with a job selling trinkets. When I recalled that Julian only made twenty-four CUCs per month, I realized that a profit of even two CUCs per day from tourists like me would be more than enough to keep them solvent, especially if they still lived with their families.

It was not yet time to round up the Korean dentists and herd them back to the bus, so I strolled the short distance back to José Marti square. The golden afternoon light, intensified by passing fleets of cumulus, helped as I photographed some of the city's architectural treasures. The first building that caught my eye was the Theatro Tomas Terry: a splendid neo-classic construction from the 19th century. As in so many places in Cuba, there was a lone figure standing outside the theater, waiting for me to show a little more interest. As I clicked what I hoped were dramatic pictures, the figure, clad all in black, approached me, smiling.

"You like to see inside?" he said. "I am certificated guide and I can show you the theater. Is even more impressionating inside."

"How much does a tour cost? I only have fifteen minutes," I said, sounding like a total philistine.

"Is only two dollars for a private tour and last how long you want – thirty minutes, ten minutes, whatever." Funny how the word whatever has caught on among non-English-speaking people.

It was a great deal for us both, because the "certificated" guide turned out to be an out-of-work actor who knew the theatre like the back of his hand. The interior is truly glorious, with intricate flower paintings on the walls. The ceiling frescoes in the lobby and in the auditorium are also most impressive, harking back to a not-so-distant past, when public taste was self-confident and eternally Roman.

"Have you worked in this theater?" I asked my guide.

"Oh yes, but is closed for a year, so no work. Maybe better in 2010." he said, nodding in a regretful way.

I later read that Tomas Terry, for whom the theater is named, was not a famous actor, as I had assumed, but a multimillionaire Cuban of Spanish-Irish extraction, who was known as "the Cuban Croesus". When he died in Paris in 1886, he was one of the richest men in the world. It should probably not have surprised me that Terry had started his business career in Cuba by buying up sick slaves, restoring them to health, and then selling them again at a considerable profit. Apart from its charming side, the colonial period has a lot to answer for.

I had spent my allotted time in the theater, however, and now my quick walking tour of colonial facades surrounding the main square had to include scanning the horizon for the Koreans. Fortunately, I spotted them in a side street within three minutes, once again playing stickball with a group of older teens. The Cubans were, again, graciously letting their oriental guests take turns at bat. I had to smile at the irony of it all; the Koreans, who already had so much in the way of material wealth and world experience, were having the time of their lives playing stickball in the streets of Cienfuegos. But it was time to go, so I summoned up my loudest whistle, whereupon they fist-bumped their hosts and jogged over to my side.

At 5 p.m. we piled into our bus and started our drive back to Havana. When we'd left the city streets behind us, Berta switched on her microphone. Were we satisfied with our stop in Cienfuegos, she wanted to know.

"Yesssss, siiii," we shouted back in unison.

"Where you wanna go now?" she asked.

"Santiago", "Trinidad", "Casa de la Trova" were the answers.

The Koreans at last realized we were playing a request game and shouted, belatedly, "Play baseball. Yeah!" Baseball had proved to be their major point of contact with Cubans.

It didn't take long for dusk to encroach. Our driver deftly guided us past meandering bikes, ox carts and farmers on horseback, all riding or driving with no light whatsoever, as we followed the long and pot-holed road back to Havana. The bus passengers, who had become a group of friends, spent the time chatting and sharing packets of Cuban crackers, sweets and plantain chips bought at the street market in Cienfuegos.

When we reached Havana at around 9 p.m. I asked to be dropped off at the Hotel Nacional. Carolina and her two friends were actually staying there, since they were in Cuba for the film festival, so the four of us got off together. We hugged and exchanged email addresses and promised to send each other pictures, but of course it didn't happen. That's just the way things go with a holiday tour: you feel close, have unforgettable experiences together, but when you get home you kind of sober up and feel silly about contacting people with pictures when they obviously took so many themselves.

I let myself in through the familiar wrought iron gate of Magdalena's building and surged up the nine flights with my overnight bag hanging from my shoulder. It felt good to be back home, climbing up my dark stairwell. When I let myself in, Magdalena was sound asleep in the living room, the TV blaring. I tried to wake her by calling her name, but was afraid she'd have a heart attack if I touched her or shouted. Since turning off the TV didn't work either, I gave up and went to bed.

As I settled down for a long night's sleep, a thousand images from the past three days floated through my head. I must have been asleep for an hour or so, when suddenly my bedroom door flew open, the light over my bed flashed on and a voice screeched, '*O, estas aqui! O, que pena, que pena!*' ("Oh, you're here. Oh, I'm sorry, Excuse me!") Then the light was snapped off and the door was pulled to. My heart still thudding from the shock of being woken, I rolled over, smiled affectionately, and went back to sleep.

11
ALONE IN HAVANA

AFTER MY TOURS WERE OVER, I had plenty of time to look around Havana on my own. One of my first stops was a makeshift drinks stand perched on the edge of the sidewalk about twenty feet down the street from Magdalena's. A young man was standing behind a little counter-on-wheels, a very old man seated beside him.

"*Buenos*," I greeted him. *Tiene cerveza y zumo de naranja*? I wanted to make sure he had beer and orange juice for me to take back to Magdalena's later in the day.

"*Si si*," he assured me. "*Todo – uno CUC*," and held up one finger.

"Fine, I'll come later," I said, then added, "Is he your grandfather?"

"Yes, he's here with me till my mother comes home at two."

"Why are you here and not down on the corner?" I asked.

"We live here," he answered, "behind those trees." I peered into a densely overgrown hollow – right across from the Hotel Nacional – that I'd been wondering about.

He told me the land was too wet and soft to support big buildings, so his family had been allowed to live there for generations. They kept chickens, he said, which explained why I always heard a rooster crowing from about four in the morning. The whole thing was so typically Cuban: the young man giving eldercare while he worked; a small farm allowed to exist in the middle of a city; the tiny, non-flourishing business.

When I went to Havana Vieja, I felt drawn at first to places I'd been to with Julian, remembering what we'd done and where we'd gone, just to prove to myself that I could get there on my own. I went back to the Cathedral, hoping to climb the bell tower, but, once again, it was closed. I ordered myself a guava juice at the El Patio, sitting at a table on the square, people-watching. Without Julian to chat with, I paid more attention to people's appearance. I noticed that many Cuban women wore colorful, shape-revealing clothes that showed off their bodies, but that Cuban men tended to wear relatively drab, loose fitting clothes; everyone seemed dressed for leisure rather than work, but it may be that more formally dressed workers escaped my survey because they were working.

Then I walked down Calle Obispo, past the man with the two phlegmatic dachshunds in rebel uniforms, and said hello. He said I could take a photo for free, which I did just to be polite. But who could I show it to in Switzerland? They'd all be upset at the incontrovertible evidence of cruelty to animals.

While having lunch at La Marina I couldn't help

overhearing an English-speaking couple at a nearby table. Judging from their accent, Tilley hats, khaki outfits and sturdy sandals, they were almost certainly Canadian. They were staring at the menu grimly as if they were about to be poisoned, patently suspicious of everything.

"You can't go wrong at this place," I said cheerfully, "everything's delicious.... Where are you from?"

"Calgary," they said in unison. "How about you?"

"Well, I was born in Halifax," I answered. They nodded. That was all they needed to know, I guess. Silence.

"So um how long are you staying in Havana for?" I finally ventured.

"Well, we're here to visit our daughter for Christmas. Cathy's here for a semester. She's studying international development. At Dalhousie?" answered the mother.

"Oh wow, Dal. What a great opportunity for her."

"Looks like this whole country could use some development," grumbled the father. "Cathy told us to eat at this place, but it doesn't look so great."

I had to stick up for La Marina: "Oh no, it's a really good choice, and the meals are delicious. Really. I can recommend it – it's very reasonable, and the location's perfect. Are you thinking of doing some sightseeing this afternoon?"

"Don't know yet – maybe. We'll probably take a taxi back to our hotel and wait for her to pick us up. She can speak Spanish," was the answer.

I wished them well. Whatever you do, I thought as I turned my attention to ordering, don't try to make contact with any Cubans by yourselves. You never know what might happen – you might actually get to know somebody. I guess those particular Canadians had just come to visit their precious daughter and had zero interest in the country and its culture. Maybe I would have behaved like that too if I'd come to a country I didn't want to be in, didn't know anything about, and thought was backward and possibly hostile. I had to revise my picture of Canadians as being friendly and tolerant, though.

After lunch I'd had enough of doing the things I'd already done with Julian and decided to strike out on my own to visit some of the places that I'd highlighted in my guidebook. I walked up the street called Teniente Rey towards the Capitolio building, where we'd started the ANGLO conference a week before. It was a narrow street with a few repainted US cars parked in it, but for all intents and purposes a pedestrian zone, just like Obispo. Behind and to the left of the Capitolio was the Partagas Cigar Factory, an ancient brick and wood building with a self-advertising billboard on its roof.

I walked into near-darkness through the wagon-wide doorway and was immediately engulfed in the sweet, damp, tangy smell of tobacco. This was the place I'd decided to visit. I paid my ten CUCs and joined a Scandinavian family of four on the forty-five minute factory tour, led by a young man who looked like a student. We started off with the already aged and fermented tobacco coming into the factory in bales from drying warehouses like those I'd seen in Vinales. Continuing from there, we followed it through all the process stages that result in a box of cigars. I'd never heard of the key step of tobacco sorting, which here at Partagas was carried out by experienced older women. We watched three of them, seated like three witches on wooden boxes and low chairs in a small, dimly lit room, sorting huge piles of tobacco leaves according to smell and texture. The guide explained that these women decide which leaves are good enough to become the thin silky wrapper on the cigar's outer surface, which leaves will end up rolled inside and which will be the binders – the ones holding the inner leaves in a tight roll. The women were chatting quietly with each other while they worked – casually sniffing, feeling, examining – seemingly oblivious to the tourists passing by ten feet away.

Moving on, we followed our guide, who spoke native-like English, over uneven wooden floors stained and softened by decades of contact with tobacco, up stairways with chipped steps and shaky handrails, past rooms full of tobacco bales waiting for either sorting or rolling. To an outsider it seemed worse than chaotic, but our guide knew where he was going and we followed, wide-eyed and obedient. How could a billion-dollar industry be based on conditions like these? How could factories that were as seemingly inefficient and sprawling as this one turn a profit?

The next important step after leaf sorting is the actual rolling of the cigars. The location for this was a large "classroom", in which forty or fifty workers sat in rows all facing in the same direction, rolling cigars at their stained and scar-worn desks. The workers were young men and women, casually dressed in jeans and T-shirts, and as they worked they listened to a person sitting at what would have been the teacher's desk, reading into a microphone.

According to our guide, a designated reader-worker reads from a newspaper in the morning and from a work of literature in the afternoon, the latter being the reason for the cigar brands Romeo y Julieta and Monte Cristo, which are actually made in a number of different cigar factories in Cuba. It was enlightening to see Cuban ideals of equality and self-improvement in action.

Each cigar roller performed steady, well practiced movements: selecting the pre-sorted filler leaves and rolling them tightly in the binder leaf, trimming the ends, fitting this cigar core into a press to set, and, finally, after half an hour in the press, putting on the supple outer leaf or wrapper that gives the cigar its color and smooth appearance. It was mesmerizing to watch, especially the way the rollers deftly trimmed away the excess tobacco leaf with a short, oval blade. Most of the time they ignored the tourists watching them, but every so often their eyes would slide sideways to take us in. That was the job they performed day in, day out. I wondered if at night their hands dreamt of rolling cigars or if they ever lost the smell of tobacco that permeated the entire factory and must have permeated them, too.

The cigar-rolling "classroom" was the high point of the tour. Even though we might previously have envisioned Carmen rolling cigars on her thigh, we now knew the truth about where hand-rolled cigars came from. After that, it was a bit of a let-down to hear about less exciting activities, like examining the finished cigars for color, quality and consistency, putting on the trademark paper bands and, finally, boxing the cigars – all activities carried out by dexterous women, without the help of machines.

In the inevitable shop at the end of the tour, cigars of all sizes and prices were on sale, from cellophane-wrapped singles to boxes. I bought three singles to take home to Switzerland as novelty gifts, but the Swedish father in our group bought two whole boxes, no doubt at a considerable saving.

My next destination, I decided, would be the Museo de la Revolucion. I knew it was nearby but had to ask where, so I mustered all my courage and stopped a military-uniformed, bearded man in the street. He answered me in Spanish without hesitating, as if there was nothing strange about my accent, which immediately put me in a good mood. The museum turned out to be just four blocks from the cigar factory. I was really beginning to enjoy being out on my own, stopping a passerby and asking directions in mediocre Spanish and then walking purposefully down a major thoroughfare to a museum, which, from its name, promised to be the holy of holies.

The Museum of the Revolution is located in the building that used to be dictator Fulgencio Batista's presidential palace, so I was expecting a certain amount of ostentation. Indeed, the sight that met my eyes was an old-style Disneyland palace, with turrets and other ornamentation, plus a crown-shaped dome on its roof. I later found out that it was decorated by Tiffany's of New York and completed in 1920. It was converted into a museum of Cuban history in the 1960s, specifically designed to celebrate the 1959 revolution.

Part of me was looking forward to seeing this

Museum. I had once been fairly enthusiastic about the Cuban revolution of 1959, and had assumed that all of Latin America would eventually follow Cuba's example. Another part of me, though, was expecting that the museum would be a repetition of the rather drab and poorly organized Che museum in Santa Clara. And indeed, the lower floors of the Havana museum do contain items like guns that belonged to famous rebels, bloodied uniforms, photos of triumphant entry in all its variations, yellowed press cuttings and other memorabilia of the revolution. Lots of photos of young, bearded men – and a few dashing revolutionary women – sitting on horseback or in the back of a jeep, smiling, laughing, celebrating the success of their endeavors.

In contrast to the general shabbiness of the revolutionary displays, one room in the museum grabbed my attention. It was the ballroom or Hall of Mirrors – *el Salon de los Espejos* – on the second floor, the balcony of which is famous as the venue of many of Fidel Castro's long-winded speeches to the nation. When I say long-winded, I mean seriously long – like four or more hours.

A Cuban wedding party was posing for photos in the famous ballroom when I entered. After they'd left, there was no one else in the room except me. I walked out onto the presidential balcony and stood all alone, looking down on the large square below, imagining it filled with thousands of cheering Cubans, imagining Fidel himself addressing the crowd from the exact spot where I now stood. A goose-bump connection with history.

For Cubans, however, the most important part of the historic display is not in the palace, but in the garden behind it. There, the visitor can walk around an outdoor pavilion displaying a number of vehicles connected with the revolution and its aftermath. First, there is the plucky little Granma, the legendary motor-launch that brought Castro and his comrades to Cuba from Mexico in 1956. It's displayed behind glass and guarded by soldiers day and night. Then, there was a large tank used in warding off the Bay of Pigs invasion and a US plane shot down in the attack, both on display as precious proof of how the new Cuba had to defend itself against *Yanqui* aggression. It was interesting to realize that, for Cubans, the Bay of Pigs invasion carries an iconic significance similar to that of the Battle of Britain or Iwo Jima in World War II. This was Cuba's finest hour, when, against all odds, it defeated the combined forces of a formidable enemy. Not totally accurate, of course, but it's an image that serves national pride and patriotism.

As I emerged from the garden, my eyes fell upon a yellow coco-taxi resting idle at the curb, its driver perched on the passenger seat, pensively spooning his lunch from a Tupperware box. Riding in a coco-taxi had been one of my fantasies since my very first day in Havana; Julian told me it would cost five CUCs – a dollar more than an ordinary taxi. Now I was ready to spring for the extra cost just to have the experience.

"*Buenos dias*," I greeted the placidly chewing driver.

"*Buenos tardes, senora*," he corrected me tactfully, while closing his plastic box, tucking it into a bag, throwing in his spoon and wiping his hands on his trousers in less than a second.

"*Quiero andar al Hotel Nacional. Cuanto es, por favor?*"

"*Hotel Nacional*? Is cos' fi' dollars," he smiled. "You wanna go now?"

"Yes, now." I conceded. So much for my native-like Spanish.

"OK, is good. Please essit here."

Thereupon he jumped out and helped me settle onto the shallow, pre-warmed seat. I kept my backpack on my back, thinking it might fall out of the half-coconut if I put it on the bench beside me. This turned out to be a major mistake, because it greatly reduced the amount of seat left for me. A coco-taxi is actually a motor scooter pulling a large, yellow, vertical hemisphere with a fairly narrow bench inside it. No handles; no seat belts. As we pulled away from the museum, I became acutely aware of just how tenuous the seating arrangements were. We first flitted down to the Malecon, swerving left and right to avoid pedestrians and parked cars, and then picked up speed on the multi-lane seaside drive, bouncing from pothole to pothole. The wind whipped through my hair as I braced my feet to maintain my perch, doing everything in my power to avoid falling forward into the road or onto the driver's back. To make matters worse, the driver turned around from time to time to comment on the scenery, prompting me to adopt a fixed, insouciant smile while my fingers vice-gripped the edge of the seat. The whole ordeal lasted about ten minutes – maybe less – but it felt like half a lifetime. I was relieved when it was over, to say the least, and my thirst for coco-taxis was quenched forever.

Being on my own in Havana also meant that I had more time to spend in the apartment, talking to Magdalena. My sub-fluent Spanish meant that these conversations stayed on a rather simple level, but we were able to communicate. Once in a while Magdalena would let off steam with a good tirade against the Castros or against the incompetence of their supporters, but most of the time she stuck to the basics so that I could follow and add to my knowledge of present-day Cuba.

She told me that her food store or *bodega* was located in the ground floor of the FOCSA skyscraper, three blocks away. Like everyone else, she had a ration booklet or *libreta* that showed what she was entitled to and what she had already claimed. She had to stand in line for certain basic food items and could also buy fruit and vegetables at very low, subsidized prices – however, they were often not available. The ration book entitled her to food for two people, herself and her granddaughter, eleven-year-old Ana Paula, who was registered as living with her. This entitled Magdalena to soy yogurt and powdered milk, which, as an adult, she would not normally be able to get. In fact, Ana Paula really only came to her grandmother's for her main meal after school in the afternoons, and was then picked up by her mother after work in the evening. This arrangement allowed Magdalena a better supply of food, which she partly passed on to her daughter's household in the form of a delicious home-cooked dinner, picked up by her daughter when she came to fetch Ana Paula.

Magdalena's daughter had a degree in chemistry and physics, so by rights she should have been working in a lab or teaching high school. But she was doing neither of these things, because she'd found a sales job in a souvenir shop in one of the big hotels in Miramar and was therefore earning a salary in CUCs. This meant that she probably supported Magdalena, too.

Magdalena was always wiping the surfaces in her kitchen with a dishcloth. In my opinion she did this automatically, whether things needed wiping or not, possibly because she couldn't see well enough to wipe according to need. She wiped her two fridges in order to remove the overnight salt build-up that came in on the sea air through her glassless kitchen windows. All of this was understandable, but why was she constantly wiping the sink draining board under the dish-rack? Was she a compulsive wiper?

"It's because of the monitors," she explained. "They just turn up and want to spray everything in the kitchen."

"What monitors?" I wanted to know, picturing men in white spacesuits, holding giant spray guns.

"The mosquito monitors," she said, as if everybody knew about them. "They can turn up at any time. They patrol the building and if they detect any mosquito babies – or even any standing water in your apartment – they have to spray it with chemicals."

"But I... I haven't seen any mosquitoes here."

"No, of course there aren't any because I wipe away the water. But if there were," she justified, "... if there were, then they'd spray and that would be very bad for my eyes."

The idea of a mosquito patrol was interesting. It was true, I realized, I hadn't noticed any mosquitos in

Cuba, not in Trinidad, not in Vinales, although I knew that other places in the Caribbean were infested. It's the sort of public health measure that a dictatorship can enforce, but only with the goodwill and understanding of the population. Keeping Cuba mosquito-free was a real achievement of the Castro regime.

Magdalena had mentioned her eyes, so I seized the opportunity to ask what was wrong with them. She told me she had *retinosis pigmentosa*, a deterioration of the retina that leads to tunnel vision and, eventually, blindness. She'd had three operations already, she said, but they hadn't really helped. She told me she used to work as a librarian in the medical library of Havana University and that she had looked up her condition in many books, but there didn't seem to be a cure.

One morning over a late breakfast together, I haltingly described – with a little help from my dictionary – what I'd so far done and seen on my own or with Julian. My excursions all met with her approval, but she wanted to hear the exact menus of what we'd eaten and the names of all the museums, squares and restaurants we'd visited. She seemed to be revisiting old memories of better days, although when I tried to show her pictures stored on my digital camera she wasn't too interested; she just couldn't see details in pictures that small.

As we drained our cups, she said *"Espera"* and shuffled off towards her end of the apartment, returning with a fading brown and white photograph, which she placed before me on the table. It showed a young girl of about eight years with a big floppy bow in her glossy hair. She was sitting on a horse in front of a wooden building that might have been a barn.

"That's me when I was a girl," she said.

"Oh, you had a horse?" I enquired.

"*Si, si*, that was my horse. Chiquita – she was called Chiquita. I rode her to school."

"To school? Was the school far from your house?"

"*Si, si*. My father had a cattle ranch in Matanzas province, so the school was some distance – five or six kilometers."

"And did you ride to school alone?"

"No, with my brothers. I had three brothers – I was the only girl. They're all dead now."

"Oh, I'm sorry... that's a pity. And what happened to the ranch?"

She laughed without smiling. "All gone after the revolution. Gone, gone, gone. The ranch land was divided up for farmers. My brothers lost everything – *todo, todo, todo*." She made a flat, wiping motion with her hand as she said this.

I sat there looking at the picture, searching for something positive to say. "You were a very pretty little girl," I said finally, "and you have beautiful handwriting – even today. It was a good school."

Magdalena dismissed this with a shrug of her shoulders, and got up to wash the dishes. She'd experienced a great deal of calamity in her seventy-odd years – certainly much more than I had in my life. She'd moved from living on a ranch to living in Havana, which before the revolution was the sophisticated pleasure capital of the Caribbean. She'd married, had three children, lived through the ups and downs of the revolution, then lived on through further privations and discomforts, fear and austerity, losing her brothers, her husband and, recently, one daughter along the way. Having nice handwriting was pretty cold comfort.

12
THE LAST OF
THE MOJITOS

I N THE DARK BEFORE DAWN, I lay thinking about
what I wanted to do and say on my last day in Cuba.
Julian had promised to return to Havana so that
we could spend another day together before I flew back
to Switzerland. I now realized how much his promise
had affected the week I'd spent alone. Everything I'd
experienced, wherever I went – Vinales, Trinidad, Santa
Clara, the Havana museums – was stored away so that I
could share it with him today and hear his comments. I
wanted to tell him about talking to the cowboys in Vinales,
and the Canadian tourists I'd observed everywhere I
went. I wanted to check Bertha's explanations with him,
tell him about touring with Linda and Carolina, the
Mexicans and the Koreans. I wanted to confess that I'd
taken a coco-taxi without waiting for him. That I'd made
friends with the sidewalk drinks-seller down the block,
and visited him for half an hour's chat every afternoon.
My head was bursting with memories collected over my
week of being a lone tourist.

Beyond all those vivid experiences, I wanted to make sure I thanked him properly for all the time he'd spent with me and for his help and advice.

At 6 a.m. the phone rang in the kitchen, just outside my room. Luckily, I was awake and could jump out of bed and grab it before Magdalena was roused by its ringing. It was of course Julian, phoning from a payphone in the central bus station in Havana. Some twenty minutes later, I went downstairs to unlock the gated entry and let him in. He'd left Santa Clara after midnight and arrived in Havana at five; then he'd waited till he thought I'd be awake. As usual, the bus had been full and he wasn't able to buy a return ticket; he'd have to take a collective taxi to get back to Santa Clara within twenty-four hours – a whole day in which he would not sleep properly or lie down at all. It was a wonderful present for me, but must have cost him a lot of cash, sleep and comfort. I could at least compensate him for the cash part.

I made tea, then sat with Julian in my room, where we caught up with each other's news in murmured conversation until I heard stirrings from Magdalena's side of the apartment. At this, I sent Julian to my bathroom to shave and freshen up after his overnight bus ride before Magdalena could entangle him in one of her stories. Seconds later she appeared in the kitchen and first went through three minutes of solemn fridge-wiping before starting to make her typical Cuban breakfast of melted-cheese-and-ham rolls with black coffee. While doing this, she and I went through the familiar steps of what had become our morning conversational routine.

"Esther (still my name, after two weeks), did you sleep well?"

"Oh yes. Very well. And you?"

"Very well also. What will you have for breakfast?"

"Tea – I've already made it, thanks."

"Would you like yogurt? Some papaya juice?"

"Yes, that would be nice. Thank you."

"And Julian? I think he arrived, didn't he?" I had a vision of Julian shaving ultra-slowly in my bathroom to gain some extra moments of relative quiet before entering the kitchen, but I couldn't avoid telling her any longer.

"Yes. He phoned before six."

She went on preparing things, lighting the gas stove, boiling water, setting the table, all the while humming contentedly to think that Julian, the kindest man she'd ever met, was back in her apartment and about to join us for breakfast. Just as I did, Magdalena appreciated Julian as a man of noble principle and as a gentleman who listened to her politely and comforted her when she complained. And the latter she did to the hilt. She fiercely resented living under the surveillance of zealous pro-regime nincompoops, who weren't even capable of repairing elevators.

When our guest finally emerged from my bedroom, smelling of soap and toothpaste, Magdalena's face brightened, a tender smile spreading from her mouth to her dimmed eyes, as she welcomed him back and invited him to take a seat at the little kitchen table. He'd brought us presents: coffee and cheese for Magdalena and a kilo of guavas for me to take back to Switzerland. She asked him about his trip to Havana, his answer prompting tirades on Cuba's precarious transport conditions and on why people such as herself could never hope to travel and visit their grandchildren again.

Julian listened politely and added a half-sentence when he got the chance. I spooned up my soybean yogurt and drank my papaya juice in happy silence, secretly pleased at how much of their Spanish I could understand after less than two weeks. Then Julian switched the topic to current events.

"By the way, Heather, do you know that you are here at a very historic time? It's ehm it's almost exactly fifty years since the Cuban revolution." He then translated this for Magdalena and added, "Magdalena, did you see the Russian ship come into Havana harbor this week?"

"*Si si,*" she answered, "it was on television last night. They fired off a cannon for each year since the revolution. Fifty years and fifty shots."

I suddenly felt involved: "Yes, I saw it. I was riding in a taxi along the Malecon yesterday morning and I saw the ship and the flash and heard the boom when the cannon fired, but I didn't know what it was. I thought it was practice for war." It was true. I couldn't believe my eyes when I saw those flashing naval cannon go off so close to the city.

"No, heh heh, the Russians are here to help Cuba celebrate. It's a pity you are leaving this evening. I think there will be some big celebrations in Havana."

When breakfast and conversation had lasted long enough, Julian said, "Well, Magdalena, thank you so much for this excellent – really excellent – breakfast, but Heather and I have some important things to do today," and rose from the table, carrying his dishes to the sink. After putting on sunhats and packing bottles of drinking water, I slipped Julian a wad of CUCs for the day's expenses, and we were off.

Since it was Sunday, and therefore not a working day, we decided to chance another bus ride to the center, taking the same bus that stopped on La Rampa, at the bottom of Magdalena's street. However, even on Sunday, the bus was extremely crowded, offering only inches of wedging-room in an already packed aisle. It got us to the old town in ten minutes, though. After a brief stroll of reminiscence round the Plaza de la Catedral, and a quick check of my email at ETECSA, where, as always, a security agent recorded my passport details, we decided to revisit the rooftop café of the Ambos Mundos hotel. Its cage-like elevator whisked us up six stories to brilliant sunshine, freshly pressed pineapple juice and panoramic views of Havana, including the old forts and a surprisingly big statue of Christ on the other side of the harbor. We stood side by side with our elbows on the rooftop wall, staring across.

"We haven't been over there yet,' I said. 'I'd love to see all those places across the harbor."

"Mhm. Well then, I think the only thing you can do is come back to Cuba again."

His answer took me by surprise – I really hadn't meant to hint at returning. But it also emboldened me to ask, "Would you come to Havana again and show me some more? I know from the past week that I enjoy sightseeing much more when I do it with you."

"Sure I would," Julian answered without hesitating. "Heh, heh, I'm looking forward to it already."

I needed some last-minute presents to take home, but was surprised to find that all the usual tourist shops – even the art market – were closed because it was Sunday. Since my plan had included buying a couple of last-minute T-shirts, Julian suggested visiting the Havana Club Rum Museum, which was open and had its own shop. However, on that particular Sunday morning the shop of the *Museo del Ron Havana Club* was filled with dozens of boisterous Russian sailors dressed in their white tropical uniforms and peaked-caps. They were obviously eager to help their Cuban comrades celebrate the fiftieth anniversary of Castro's revolution and even more eager to drink a toast or two in rum. Thus, the shop was filled to bursting with sailors buying rum and anything else offered for sale. Julian and I decided to tour the museum first and put off shopping till the sailors had left.

Havana Club tours are offered in a variety of languages, but for some obscure reason Julian and I were assigned a Cuban guide who gave tours in French. We did not protest, but accepted it, like so many last-minute "adjustments" in Cuba, with a smile. For me, French was much easier to understand than Spanish or Russian. The first highlight of the tour was a model of a realistic-looking 19th century sugar mill where a tiny train chugged around a track, bringing sugar cane to be pressed for cane juice, then reduced to molasses and fermented in huge cast-iron vats. Julian and I nodded enthusiastically whenever our guide seemed to have doubts about our comprehension. We followed him further, nodding and smiling like polite fools, past vats of bubbling molasses and through a cobwebby cellar full of barrels.

We could hear Russian groups ahead of us, plowing through the tour in raucous tones. This was because the second highlight of the tour is the chance to get a free taste of Havana Club rum, served in an old-time bar. Due to our eagerness to claim our Havana Club reward before the Russians had drunk it all, Julian and I refrained from asking any questions. Alas, however, when we arrived at the endpoint, the bar was packed with large, fair-haired men in white, knocking back glass after glass of the good stuff. Not a chance of getting anywhere near the bar. So after buying a couple of T-shirts in the shop, we exited to the street and made our way for the last time to our restaurant, where we consoled ourselves with lunch and cold beer, amid a Sunday gathering of Cuban families.

———

When we got back to Vedado, Magdalena offered us some of her flan, which she was having for dessert. We sat down around the kitchen table and told her about our race for the rum with the Russian sailors. She seemed to enjoy the story, and it occurred to me that she might enjoy going out for a farewell drink that afternoon. I knew from some of her questions that, although she lived right across the street from the Hotel Nacional, she hadn't been there for ages. So after I'd paid her for two weeks of bed and breakfast, and thrown the few things I hadn't given away into my suitcase, I persuaded Magdalena to come with us for a farewell *mojito*. She resisted at first, saying she couldn't see and couldn't walk, but I reasoned that if she could see and walk well enough to go grocery shopping alone in the FOCSA building three blocks away, she could easily make it across the street to the Nacional. Finally, she gave in and agreed to come with us for a drink. She disappeared into her bedroom for twenty minutes and emerged wearing high-heeled mules, navy-blue slacks, a sleeveless top, a chiffon scarf, blue eye shadow and lipstick. Julian and I were stunned but said not a word.

The shoes, combined with her poor eyesight, meant she had to take our arms and walk slowly, but she held her head high as we made our way past the row of palms and through the hotel lobby, walking shoulder-to-shoulder and arm-in-arm, like Siamese triplets, to the garden lounge on the far side of the lobby. Once there, we plumped down into one of their luxuriously cushioned couches and ordered our *mojitos*.

Magdalena had been silent on the way, perhaps because she had to concentrate on walking. Now she seemed to relax a little and take note of her surroundings. As usual, a trio of local musicians moved from table to table, playing the songs they thought all tourists wanted to hear: *Guantanamera, Una Gardenia* and Love Me Tender. An ocean breeze swept up over the Malecon and rustled the palm fronds overhead. It was time to say my bit. I asked Julian to translate for me.

"Thank you so much, Magdalena and Julian, for a wonderful time in Cuba," I started. "You've been so kind to me, so welcoming, so patient. A hotel can be very nice, but I'm really happy I lived with you, Magdalena, and had someone to talk to in the morning and evening. I've learned so much about life in Cuba from you. And, Julian, as I've already said, you showed me Havana and explained everything and, and... well, you really made me love Cuba and its people."

"There's nothing to thank – I enjoyed every minute with you," answered Julian, after he had translated what I'd said for Magdalena. "And I am sad now because I will miss going around Havana with you, but I'm also happy because there's so much more to see, and you have promised you will return."

"And you, Magdalena," Julian said in Spanish, "are you glad you came to the Hotel Nacional with us to say goodbye?"

Magdalena squeezed my hand to express her immediate feelings, but said nothing for a long time. I sensed she had already gone beyond our fond farewells and was thinking of something far sadder. She took a long sip from her *mojito*, holding the perspiring glass in a handkerchief.

"I said I didn't want to come to the Nacional because I couldn't imagine how it would be after all the years," she finally murmured, looking around at the graceful lawns and comfortable furniture. "But it's still beautiful – I'm glad I came. I haven't been here since before my husband died, and that was forty years ago."

13
BETWEEN VISITS

Dear Heather,

By now, you have been gone ten days. I hope your trip back to Zurich was comfortable, and that you are well. Your words of appreciation on the last day made me very happy. Before you arrived, I was worried that you wouldn't like life in Cuba. But now I know that you enjoyed your trip very much…

Dear Julian,

Thank you so much for making my stay in Havana 100% enjoyable. Your patience, organization and guidance were more than I could have hoped for. I tell every one of my friends and family what a great time I had in Cuba. Your country has a very special charm, but you added so much. You and Magdalena made me feel very welcome. From the first day I felt as

> if I was among friends. I hope we can keep
> in touch for a long time…

My first visit to Cuba had made a huge impression on me. Through conversations with Julian and through listening to Magdalena's rants and stories, I had begun to get an idea of what life there was like. It seemed that Cubans were living in a condition of constant hardship and scarcity, but had developed strategies to cope with it. There also appeared to be little corruption in government – at least there were no obviously rich people. And Cubans expected fairness. However, the price of this fairness was constant vigilance, as the government's hand was exceedingly firm. My visit had also led to a new phase in my relationship with Julian, one in which we discussed personal concerns and reported details of daily life that had nothing to do with teaching. I wrote him at least three letters or emails a month, sending the emails to his son's account at the medical university. Julian wrote to me just as often, but usually hand-written letters, as he was not well versed in computers. The letters still took three to six weeks to arrive.

> Dear Heather,
> Yesterday, on a TV program, I heard something said by an excellent Cuban film-maker. "…ese tragico y maravilloso sentido de lo efimero" (that tragic and wonderful sense of the ephemeral). This is something I always have in mind: Ephemeral things are tragic because they

are never repeated, but they are wonderful because they may be kept in memories in our brain, and they may be recollected as many times as we wish. For example, this is the wonderful side of the days we spent together in Havana... The tragic side is that they will not be repeated exactly the same anymore.

Julian had told me he'd enjoyed spending the time with me, but I hadn't fully realized the role I played in his memory and imagination. It was true: over the two weeks I'd spent in Havana, our relationship had evolved into a close friendship. We were not in any way romantically involved, but we both cared about what happened to the other in the way that family and best friends do.

Besides bringing us closer together, our written communication also revealed aspects of daily life that were hard to observe. For example, when I asked him how he would celebrate his birthday, Julian wrote:

> ... I will tell you something that perhaps will surprise you: I've only had one birthday party in all of my life. It was in Mexico, in 2000. I was teaching English to a group of employees from a state institution, and they learned when my birthday was through a Cuban colleague. Then they organized a party in an elegant restaurant in town.... They also gave me some presents. I will never forget that

day, because it was something completely unusual and very touching in my life. As you know, in Cuba we have been having a hard time for almost five decades, and birthday parties are not affordable for most people. What we do is give some small birthday presents, but not parties.

I knew that Julian valued books above other possessions, and I also knew from our time together that he liked nothing more than to browse the shelves of second-hand book dealers. What I discovered through our correspondence was how this love started:

> At the age of 9, I was a very thin boy... I was very shy and took refuge in reading. I began reading all printed material that was available – books, magazines and newspapers. At that age I became familiar with the political situation in Cuba and the Korean War and also began to read the Gospels. Later on when I became a teacher at the age of 19, the first thing I did when I got my first salary was to go to a bookstore and buy 100 pesos of books...

Knowing how much he loved books, I wanted to send him some, but it turned out to be harder than expected. Internet book suppliers wouldn't send books to a Cuban address due to the US embargo, so I had them sent to my address and then mailed them to him myself. In 2009, a book I'd sent to Julian disappeared in the hands of the Cuban postal service. The probable theft upset him, and he seemed more surprised than I was that such a thing should happen. He told me it would be safer in future to address parcels to his pastor, Nelson, care of the church.

I found out that I could actually send small parcels to Cuba fairly easily and cheaply via Canada Post. So I asked Julian if there were any small, light items besides books that he or his family needed but couldn't buy in Cuba. There were many – and they were things I wouldn't necessarily have predicted: typewriter ribbon, flea collars, multivitamins, laxatives, painkillers, disposable razors, anti-histamines, pens and herbal tea. So every four months, when I visited Halifax, I filled a small box with items for Julian and his family and addressed it care of Pastor Nelson at his church in Santa Clara.

Thus it was that Nelson became our parcel link. An energetic and friendly young minister with many foreign contacts, Nelson came to Europe every year to attend workshops and generally set up more contacts between his three Cuban congregations and congregations in Europe. I first met him in June 2009, in a town near Zurich, where he was staying as the guest of a Swiss pastor. He turned out to be a chubby, short, very dark Afro-Cuban, bubbling with smiles and laughter, and highly communicative in Spanish or rudimentary English. He called everyone brother or sister – *hermano* or *hermana* – so when he met me, he said:

"I am very happy to meet you, *hermana* Heather. My friend Julian has mentioned your name often."

"And I've heard a lot about you from Julian, too," I smiled back, meeting his eyes.

"Only good things I hope," he shot back, with a mock-worried grimace followed by uproarious laughter.

Nelson and I sat and talked in the pastor's garden. I heard about his church projects in Cuba, about contacts and experiences in Germany, about how much Julian helped him with English contacts. When I handed him a parcel of clothes and medications to take to Julian's family, he accepted it without batting an eye, promising it would be delivered. When I gave him money for his church, he put his hand on his heart and blessed me. Then he suddenly remembered something and, saying *un momento*, dashed into the house. Two minutes later he returned with a book-shaped object wrapped in brown paper.

"Is from Julian," he panted. "I forget almost," and then he laughed and tapped his head. I unwrapped an English translation of José Marti's biography.

Nelson was a genius at meeting people and speaking to congregations. The day I met him, the local Swiss pastor had invited him to attend the Sunday service to tell the congregation about his church in Santa Clara. The Swiss minister said he would help by translating from Spanish to German.

"No problem," answered Nelson. "Do I speak ninety seconds, ten minutes or thirty minutes?"

"Five minutes," said the Swiss.

So at the appointed time, Nelson stood at the front

of a Swiss church he'd never seen before and in rapid-fire Spanish extemporized on his work in Cuba, while his Swiss host translated. He described groups he'd started, like the seniors' club, nursery school, classes for adults and his music program for teenagers as well as visits from American, Canadian and German church groups. When he stopped, he got a standing ovation from the Swiss congregation – the first ovation that church had ever seen. And the talk had taken exactly five minutes.

Nelson and the Swiss pastor had met at a workshop in Berlin, where they were discussing how to get people to interact more with their fellow humans. It was Nelson who suggested hugging people instead of shaking their hands, as a way of getting closer and thus breaking through barriers of untouchability. His ideas were radical, but founded on personal experience and reflection.

Left alone together in the garden, Nelson and I started to chat about our lives in a mixture of Spanish and English. He soon mentioned that he was in love with a young woman from his church in Santa Clara, but that their relationship was a secret. Hearing this, I remembered Julian's story about the Cuban mother who had nearly starved herself to death because her daughter wanted to marry a Black pastor.

"Why is it a secret?" I asked, trying to sound naïve.

"Her mother is against a marriage," he said, "because I am dark."

"Maybe you could give her a hug?" I suggested, only half seriously, whereupon Nelson roared with laughter at the idea.

He was still chuckling when he said, "Yes, I will try it."

In the summer of 2009, six months after we'd met in Havana, Julian retired from teaching. The Cuban parliament had passed a new law granting educators a pension amounting to ninety percent of their final salary; Julian was sixty-five and decided to take the plunge. He retired in July, and received his first monthly pension of 550 Cuban pesos ($22) that August. He would be able to supplement that with "part-time contracts" as a university teacher of English, but, as he wrote,

> ...I would also like to have more time to
> look after my mother, read, watch films
> and do some translation work.

He very much believed that he should do the lion's share of work in taking care of his 94-year-old mother, who lived in their household and was by this time suffering from Alzheimer's.

Since he was retiring, an end-of-semester retirement party was organized by his department at the medical university. Julian looked forward to it for several weeks, planning what he would say to his colleagues in his farewell remarks. Unfortunately, however, the party had to be cancelled at the last minute because no refreshments of any kind were available.

> These days all resources have been given
> to the organizers of the "Carnival" held
> for three days in the city, where they sell

food, beer and sweets, surrounded by
noisy pop music… and at night, parades
and floats.

The Carnival, he told me, is a public celebration
invented by the government and held in the hot summer
season, when people tend to take their vacation. It's
understood as a replacement for the unobserved
Christmas festivities.

———— ••• ————

Retirement, Julian thought, would also give him more
time for English-Spanish interpreting when groups from
the US, Canada and Europe visited churches in Cuba.
On these visits, he would often accompany Nelson, who
was good at organizing exchanges with churches outside
the country, but was not particularly fluent in English.
Julian wrote:

I enjoy participating in these visits
because I get a lot of practice with the
language, am able to interact culturally
with them, and mostly, because these
visits contribute to building bridges of
friendship between peoples.

Julian also hoped his retirement would provide the
opportunity to travel a little, and was very keen to see
parts of the US and Europe for himself. He thought this
might be possible if he were allowed to accompany Nelson
as an interpreter. However, he had mixed feelings:

...traveling to another country for Cubans is a serious and complex issue that always takes a lot of effort, time, arrangements, steps and money. Sometimes this is so stressing and tiresome for the person that people prefer not to travel at all.

To illustrate this he recounted the circumstances of his trip to Britain, after he had won a British Council scholarship to attend a six-week summer course in teaching English for special purposes. Despite several costly trips to Havana for bureaucratic procedures, he received his Cuban passport so late on the hot and humid day of departure that he had only one hour to get the passport to the British Embassy for a visa. As a result, he wrote,

I had to run (I mean RUN, RUN)... and arrived there sweating, only ten minutes before the embassy closed.

After collecting his visa, he left directly for Havana airport and his flight. He did want to travel, he told me, but every time he thought about making travel arrangements, past experiences flooded his memory and he felt stressed with a kind of PTSD that also made him dread traveling. It seemed as if Cuban authorities deliberately made it difficult for Cuban citizens to go to other countries, even when the would-be traveler was not engaged in politics.

Julian also told me more about the general economic situation in Cuba. Soon after my first visit he mentioned the effects of the so-called financial crisis:

> Of course we notice the global recession. Imports have been reduced to a minimum, which is clearly reflected in the reduction of variety in shops. Besides, we are facing a shortage in staple foods like rice, sugar, and salt. Lots of people have become redundant in many workplaces and prices in the black market have gone up.

Raul Castro, who had taken over as president from his brother Fidel, was trying to steer the Cuban economy towards more efficiency by eliminating unproductive jobs. It was announced that hundreds of thousands of state workers would be let go.

> Heather, I want to thank you so much for your solidarity and kindness. Your parcel arrived after being seven weeks in the postal system. We are all very grateful for what you have sent, especially for the vitamins and medications, which contribute a lot to our health and well-being.... Is our friendship the consequence of destiny, providence or chance? We will possibly never know. What I do know is how much my life has been enriched by you, how much you have opened me and

how much welfare you have brought to
me and my family.

All the parcels I sent to Nelson's church address
arrived safely. I was only too happy to send Julian's family
over-the-counter medications, flea collars for the two
dogs, pens, T-shirts and DVDs; however, there was one
essential thing I couldn't send due to banking regulations:
money. We didn't write about it, but I felt selfish sitting on
my savings in Switzerland when they had so little. Julian's
family had no relatives in the US and no one in the tourist
industry, which meant they had no access to CUCs, the
dollar-based currency needed to buy everything beyond
the bare essentials. More than two years had passed since
I'd been in Cuba, so I decided it was time for a second
visit. Besides, I wanted to see Julian and Magdalena again,
walk the streets of old Havana, hear the rhythms of *son*,
and once more experience a uniquely Cuban way of life
that might soon disappear.

In your last email you say that you're
working on a plan to meet me again. I
got so excited by this piece of news that
I dreamed of you last night. You had
come to Santa Clara and we were walking
along the streets by night. It was like
carnival time, because there were kiosks
in the street. Then we met Jorge Luis, a
colleague of mine, and I introduced him
to you. Then you gave me a newspaper
with a crossword for me to solve and I got

afraid of not being able to solve it. And then it was THE END.

———— •••• ————

Since Havana is a short flight from Halifax, I decided to fly to Cuba from Canada, where I could combine the trip with a family visit. I obtained my Cuban visa from the same consulate villa in Bern, manned by the same staff and furnished with the same battered red furniture. But there were some differences too: there was no longer a picture of the uniformed Fidel on the consulate wall, but instead an official photograph of his brother Raul, looking benevolent in a farmer's straw hat. And this time I was neither required to have an invitation to Cuba nor even asked if I had a special reason for going. I just said I was a tourist and that was fine.

The flight from a snowy March day in Halifax to a warm and breezy, sundrenched Havana took only four hours. This time I was less nervous when I underwent the ritual ordeal at immigration. There was the same drill about taking off my glasses, but I kept my face absolutely straight and controlled all impulses to say anything. This time my rather large suitcase popped onto the luggage conveyor among the first, and there were no customs agents visible, which meant that I'd slipped into Cuba with a laptop, fifteen books, countless English teachers' magazines, a bag of apples and a watch for Julian, plus more presents for Magdalena and her grandchildren. I was elated that it had all gone so well. This time I had no doubt but that Julian would be waiting on the other side of the barrier, and in a few short seconds I crossed the cavernous customs area and threw my arms around the same tweed jacket as before.

"Welcome back to Cuba," beamed Julian, as we came out of our hug. "Well, and do you have everything – all your bags?"

"Yup, that's it – just this one big suitcase and my backpack."

We proceeded to the currency exchange desk, where I changed Canadian dollars into good old CUCs. It was early afternoon and I hadn't had anything besides a soft drink and a bag of pretzels on the Air Canada flight.

"What about getting something to eat before we take the taxi into town?" I asked, thinking that Julian was probably hungry, too.

"Yes, yes, it's a good idea. There's a cafeteria upstairs. I had a coffee there just before you came."

We took the escalator up to the mezzanine, where Julian and I ordered limp cheese sandwiches and fruit juice.

"I'm feeling quite tired," he said. "I have been awake all the night."

"Oh no, did you have to take a night bus to Havana?"

"No, no, I'm not tired from the bus, but something very terrible has happened and I had to deal with it all day yesterday – Nelson was killed."

"What? What do you mean he was killed?"

"Well, he had an accident. It was Sunday and he was driving to the church in Santa Clara from his other church in Sancti Spiritus, and his car just went off the road and hit a tree and he was immediately dead. Maybe he fell asleep while he was driving – they think so anyway."

"Oh no. This is terrible news, Julian. I'm so, so sorry."

"Yes, it's terrible for our church because Nelson had so much energy and so many contacts. Everybody was crying in Santa Clara yesterday – even the Catholics."

"So do you have to go back for the funeral this week?"

"No, no. His mother already came from Havana to get his body for burial. You know, in Cuba we don't have the refrigerated rooms that other countries have, so a dead body – or should I say a corpse? – has to be buried the day after death."

I didn't know what to say. Less than a year ago, I'd been joking with Nelson about hugging his girlfriend's mother; now he was gone. Julian probably wanted to be in Santa Clara with the rest of the Presbyterian congregation, not here in Havana trying to show me a good time.

"But Julian, don't you want to go back to Santa Clara and help with arrangements?"

Julian drank his juice down to the bottom of the bottle, then he shook his head. "No, believe me, I have thought about this and there is almost nothing to arrange. I would rather be here in Havana with you – really. I can't do anything more in Santa Clara – there's nothing anyone can do; we have to recover slowly from this tragedy and I can start to recover here with you."

I was no longer hungry, so Julian re-wrapped and pocketed the sandwiches for future reference and we went down to the taxi rank just outside the front entrance. First we took a taxi into Havana, to the *casa particular* where he was staying for ten CUCs a night. It was about six blocks from Magdalena's, and the hosts seemed friendly and welcoming. Here we unloaded all the things I had brought for Julian and his family – my old laptop, books, magazines, apples, CDs, thumb drives, a watch – from my big suitcase and left them in Julian's room. This lightened my suitcase considerably and made it much easier to roll to Magdalena's apartment, especially because my old enemy, the Otis elevator, had finally given up the ghost.

Together, we carried my suitcase up to the tenth floor, where Magdalena was waiting for us. She seemed happy to see me, even though I had made little progress in Spanish in my two years of absence. My room was exactly the same: the louvered glassless windows, the pink chenille bedspread, the clean bathroom with occasional water. I unpacked my things while Julian used Magdalena's phone to make phone calls connected with Nelson's death. He also phoned his wife to find out if there were any new developments in Santa Clara.

Needing to relax and recover, we went across the street to our "green living room", the garden of the Hotel Nacional, which was as grand as ever. We sat side-by-side in the vast hotel garden, gazing out to sea and sipping cold drinks. Little had changed.

"Are you sure you can do this, Julian?" I said. "You know, I can amuse myself for a few days while you settle whatever you have to do about Nelson's death."

"I am very sure, Heather. You are my best friend in the world, and I need you right now to take my mind off the sad events in Santa Clara."

"Yes, but…"

"Really. I am very sure."

14
COUNTING CHANGE

A T BREAKFAST, MAGDALENA NATURALLY WANTED to discuss the circumstances of Nelson's death. Nelson's car had left the road and overturned, Julian told us. He had only had his driving license for about five months, so he was a fairly inexperienced driver. The car had been bought for him by a large Presbyterian church in North Carolina.

"The Americans gave him a car?" Magdalena marveled. "He should never have started driving. Why does a priest need a car?"

"Well, he had three churches in three different towns. He had to drive from one church service to the next on Sundays," explained Julian.

"*Amor de dio* – I'm sure he was going too fast! American cars are too fast for Cuban roads," she declared, forgetting that most cars in Cuba were American and also oblivious of the fact that Nelson had been driving a Peugeot. Julian looked at me with a straight face, raising his eyebrows ever so slightly.

"His poor family!" exclaimed Magdalena. "What will they do now?"

"Well, there's only his mother," answered Julian. "She came to Santa Clara to take his body back to Havana for burial. He must be buried already."

I decided to try changing the subject to something less depressing, and started out bravely in my best Spanish: "*Magdalena, necesitas pan, o leche, o algo mas? Julian y yo, podemos comprar algo para ti...*" Julian came to my rescue: "*Ah si*, Magdalena, listen, we are going into the city today and can bring anything you need. Tell us what we should buy."

Magdalena admitted – after some persuasion – that she could use more breakfast ingredients, like bread, milk, coffee and cheese if we wanted to get them, but it was not really necessary, her daughter could get her everything she needed. We wanted to contribute to the food supply, we said, since we were eating most of it. We interpreted Magdalena's reluctant agreement as the end of the conversation and prepared to leave the apartment.

In the old part of Havana we strolled down pedestrian-zoned Obispo as we had done so often during my first visit. The two state-run bookshops were still there, as well as the tourist-trap cafés and open-air restaurants with *Buenavista Social Club* tunes belting from their sound systems.

There was at least one difference though: a pet store had opened. Julian didn't even know that such a thing as a pet store existed, and had a big grin on his face when we entered. He and his family owned two dogs, but the idea of a store aimed solely at pet owners and selling leashes and toys for dogs, as well as food especially created and packaged for dogs and other pets, was the epitome of indulgence – or possibly decadence – to him. The store was rather quiet, as there were no other customers, and the shelves were sparsely stocked. Julian greeted the owner, a woman in her thirties, and asked if she had a brush for a dog with long, fluffy hair, as their dog was constantly getting knots in its fur. She was pleased to show him several, which he examined closely, commenting on each one. After thanking her, we left without making a purchase.

"Did you see the price on that brush?" he said. "It cost eight CUCs – more than I earn in a week. I don't think she'll have much business with those prices."

In her defense I said, "Well, she probably has to import everything from Canada or Europe, so of course her prices will be too high for the average shopper here."

"Yes, but that makes me think… there must be some people here in Havana who can afford those prices. You can see how things are developing in Cuba with the two currencies side by side. Some people now have enough CUCs to spend eight dollars on a brush for their dog. Other people don't even have eight miserable pesos to spend on their dog, and that is bad."

"What do you feed Yulia and Cynthia?" I inquired.

"Oh, we give them what is left when we finish eating – or sometimes Isabel cooks rice for them." I wondered if the pet-shop woman would be able to survive long enough for consumers to catch up.

Quite soon we passed a hole-in-the-wall bakery doing a roaring business in fresh rolls, so we bought a dozen for Magdalena. This was definitely different from my previous visit, when all food sold in the street looked deadly or unappetizing, as if made from melted rubber or play-dough. We asked about a *supermercado* in the neighborhood, and were directed to an excellent and apparently booming new food shop – with prices in CUCs of course – around the corner. The clinically clean store had good cheese, eggs, yogurt and coffee, so we decided to call in later on our way home. Again, a store like this was unheard of on my previous visit.

When we got to Plaza de la Catedral, which was bathed in blinding sunlight, we decided to go into the cathedral and have a look. I had not entered churches on my first visit to Cuba because most seemed closed and because I thought – perhaps wrongly – that entering them might be regarded as a political act. This time Julian said he thought the cathedral would be an interesting place for me to see, so we entered the dark building and were almost immediately intercepted by a well-groomed young man in a suit and tie, who I assumed to be a priest-in-training. He invited us to have a free tour of the church, its statues and relics; Julian, ever open to free information, accepted, so we spent the next twenty minutes hearing about the cathedral and its history in the young man's weird, falsetto English. Two of his stories were memorable; one was about Columbus' bones and the other about the Virgin of Cobre.

Christopher Columbus, after making four round trips to the New World – which he unwaveringly believed to be China – died in Spain in 1506. His remains were eventually transferred first to Santo Domingo and later to Cuba, where they were placed in a niche next to the cathedral altar. And they might still be there today if the Spanish-American war of 1898 had not led Cubans to send the remains back to Spain for safekeeping. The "Columbus niche" in Havana cathedral is now empty, but is as revered as if the explorer's bones were still resting there.

The other story was triggered by a small, extravagantly clothed figure of the Virgin Mary, exhibited in a glass case in the cathedral nave. This is a replica of the *Virgen de la Caridad del Cobre*, whose story is as follows. In the 1600s, three boys, caught in a storm at sea and fearing for their lives, came across just such a statue of the Virgin attached to a board and floating in the waves. The storm subsided as soon as the boys fished out the statue, which – they were astounded to discover – was completely dry. Accounts of this miracle spread, and the tiny statue was installed in a shrine at El Cobre in eastern Cuba, becoming the center of a cult. Ultimately, the *Virgen de la Caridad* came to be declared the patron saint of Cuba. Julian enjoyed hearing the young man's version of two well-known stories, and was even more delighted to supply some of the English words in his narrative.

After our tour, we were given special permission to climb the right bell tower of the cathedral, which afforded an excellent view of the square below, where we'd so often enjoyed a glass of guava juice at El Patio. As we stood there alone, pointing out Havana landmarks to each other and leaning on the parapet, one or two of the huge stone blocks under our arms started rocking back and forth. After a second of frozen terror, we gingerly stepped back to safety, then helped each other down the narrow staircase to the square.

Guava juice was just the thing for frayed nerves. The taste and price hadn't changed one bit: two CUCs for a tall glass. El Patio's wrought-iron tables and chairs hadn't changed either, and there was lots of room and peace to contemplate the square of perfectly proportioned colonial buildings surrounding us: the cathedral's swirling baroque façade with its double layer of columns, and the stately mansions of the governors of Cuba, slumbering behind their shadowy arcades.

While we were sipping our juice, a man with a briefcase rushed past, then did a double-take and returned to our table to express his condolences on Nelson's death. He turned out to be an acquaintance of Julian's from Santa Clara, a man who worked for the Catholic diocese there. He mentioned something about new English courses, but I couldn't understand exactly what he said. When he'd hurried off again, Julian filled me in.

"Hmm! Do you know what? The Catholic diocese in Santa Clara is going to offer adult education courses in English from next September. And, what is even more interesting, he said they will get in touch with me about teaching one or two of the courses. That would be two or four evenings a week. Well, it's very nice of them to think of me – and of course it would be another ehm source of income. It's well paid, in fact. I'll be earning more in my retirement than I ever earned as a professor."

When our glasses were empty, we strolled the short distance to the Cathedral of San Francisco de Asis. This was not motivated by religious fervor but by the noonday sun. There appeared to be some kind of free exhibit of Cuban art in the church, so we thought we'd have a look, just to get cooled off. While we were standing in the doorway, reading posters on our way in, I couldn't help noticing a series of young women in tight jeans and skimpy tops, entering the church. They didn't look like the sort of person who would spend much time inside a cathedral, but they appeared to be carrying musical instruments: violins, cellos, bases – no doubt violas, too.

The art display inside the Cathedral of St. Francis was rather uninspiring, but the tuning sounds that emerged from the all-girl orchestra that was forming before our eyes sounded highly professional. Their conductor was a striking, short-haired blond, whom Julian recognized at once. Her name was Zenaida Romeu, he said, and she belonged to a well-known family of Cuban musicians who had been conductors and performers for generations. Suddenly the first glorious descending chords of Tchaikovsky's Serenade for Strings surged through the cathedral's high arches, and the whole nave resonated with the grandeur and transport of the music. I had to sit down and listen. How could that beautiful music be coming from these girls who, just a few minutes earlier, had slouched in like typical pop-culture know-nothings? Zenaida Romeu stopped them and corrected their phrasing, humming how she wanted it to sound. Then they started again. So much concentration, so much respect for the music, so much skill. Unfortunately, a guard reminded us that it was not a concert and we were meant to be looking at the art exhibit, so we had to enjoy our concert while standing up, facing the wall.

It was a magical experience for me, revealing Cuba at its best, and I hope in future I won't be so quick to pre-judge someone's musical skill by their appearance.

———————•••——————

A day later, Julian and I were squeezing our way down the aisle of a middle-sized Cubatur bus headed for Vinales. I was looking forward to doing a tour with him, instead of on my own. Among our fellow passengers I noticed at least five pairs of friendly Canadians, who probably wanted a change from sunbathing on the balconies of their Miramar hotels.

"Hi there, where're you guys from?" inquired one of the women, peeking over the seat in front.

"Well, he's from Cuba and I'm from Nova Scotia," I answered.

"Oh cool, from Cuba, eh?" I could see her sizing Julian up as some kind of gigolo. "Did you uh meet here in Cuba?"

"We've actually known each other for quite a while," I said drily.

"Oh, so do you live in Cuba?" she asked me, obviously trying to work out our backstory.

"No, I live in Switzerland. Julian lives in Cuba – but not in Havana – and I'm just visiting for a couple of weeks… so we're taking this tour to do something together."

"Fantastic… well, hey, have a great time then," she said, clearly disbelieving me.

The bus started and the tour guide – his name was Carlos this time – started droning into his microphone.

When we were finally barreling along the *carretera central*, Julian closed his eyes.

"Are you thinking about Nelson?" I asked him. "Are you sure you wouldn't rather be in Santa Clara?"

"No, no, not at all. As I told you, there's absolutely nothing more I can do in Santa Clara. People have taken care of everything concerning Nelson. They are grieving, yes, but I can't help them."

"But wouldn't you like time to grieve, too?"

Julian paused for a minute, then answered: "As a friend of Nelson's I am very sorry that he is gone, but as a Christian I know he is with God and that is certainly nothing bad." And then he added: "And I am very, very happy to spend these days with you. Really. You are a dear friend and you make me smile and even laugh, and that also helps me."

"OK," I said, "if that's what you really feel, I won't ask you again."

"It is, believe me. Part of my heart might be sad, but most of it wants to enjoy our precious time together."

So we rolled along under a bright March sky, commenting on the different kinds of palm trees, on the oxen dragging heavy sledges over the fields, on the road workers attempting to trim away rampant vegetation with *machetes*. The Cuban countryside seemed exactly the same as two years before: red earth, lots of vegetation – mostly wild – and bucolic scenes of non-mechanized cultivation. In fact, everything seemed the same as on my last trip to Vinales until the radiator tube blew just before Pinar del Rio. The driver pulled over to the side of the road and ran to get water from a nearby *campesino* house. With that water we hobbled on into Pinar and parked. It was going to be a walking tour for a while until another bus could be sent out to relieve our crippled vehicle, Carlos informed us.

———————•••———————

First we walked to the famous Donatien cigar factory and had the full cigar-making tour. Here, the workers were quite a bit bolder than those I'd seen in Havana: they were constantly whispering "CUC? Dollar?" through the wooden grill that separated them from us. This was highly embarrassing for Julian, who couldn't believe his fellow countrymen would lower themselves to beg in this way, when they were being paid good money to roll cigars. Carlos was waiting outside when we emerged from the inevitable cigar shop at the end of the tour. He looked strained.

"Next we go see rum factory," he announced. So we followed him, two by two like schoolchildren, down several of Pinar's side streets to a small distillery. On our way we passed a pair of astronauts in light grey overalls and rubber boots, their goggles and breathing masks hanging around their necks. In their hands they carried what looked like giant water pistols. Then it came to me.

"Julian!" I stopped in my tracks. "Are those guys mosquito monitors?"

"Heh heh, yes, you are absolutely correct," Julian smiled back at me. "They go from house to house, checking for mosquito larvae. How did you know?"

"Magdalena told me about them. I never thought I'd actually see one."

There was no explanatory tour at the distillery

because Carlos was on the phone. We were left to our own devices and allowed to wander through the various factory rooms, watching ladies clean vats of rum bottles with ancient brushes, while the male workers looked after the distilling process. A few of us tried taking artsy pictures of steamy vats and sun-rays through rum bottles. Others wasted no time with photography, but stuck close to the workers in the distilling room until they were treated to small glasses of neat rum.

Once we'd done the distillery, Carlos was at a loss. There was no relief-bus to be had and twenty tourists to entertain in a rather dull place. He was sending us off to a nearby soda fountain, while he went to find our bus and driver. Julian, to whom Carlos had murmured quick instructions in Spanish, was to be our new leader. Julian seemed happy to take over and led the way down a side-street, past a primary school playground where tiny pupils were playing soccer, unsupervised, in mixed teams. Here he stopped to answer questions on the Cuban school system before leading us onward to the soda fountain.

"Wow. I don't believe it! I haven't seen a place like this since I was a kid," crowed one of the Canadians.

"Let's see if there's a jukebox. I wanna hear the Everly Brothers." said another.

Our group settled into the vinyl-upholstered booths straight out of the sixties and ordered virtually all the cold drinks in the place. If there had been a jukebox, we would have started dancing. It was a moment of pure, unanticipated delight. There we were – Canadians, Latin Americans and Europeans – sitting together for an hour, marveling at the décor straight out of our (or our parents') youth, buying each other incredibly cheap beers and colas, trading ideas for places to go in Havana, collecting ideas for repairing a leaky radiator tube. People sang lines from Buddy Holly and Elvis Presley songs. Couples got up to demonstrate the twist and the lindy in the aisles. Julian was asked lots of questions about what things were like in Cuba in the sixties: about school, about music, about revolutionary heroes. We'd forgotten the tour completely, when our bus appeared outside the front window. Same bus, same driver, same radiator tube.

———————— •••• ————————

After lunch and a whip-through tour of photogenic Vinales, where I noticed that virtually all the bungalows now had *Pension*, B&B or For Rent signs on their verandas, our final stop was a prosperous-looking tobacco farm, where the farmer himself told us about growing and drying tobacco. I was afraid that Julian, newly popular after his stint as our guide in Pinar del Rio, might take over translating for Carlos, but instead he withdrew to the wall of the curing barn with his arms folded. After explanations, the farmer sat down at a table in the middle and rolled a cigar before our eyes. It was not exactly "round, firm and fully packed", but it was a cigar. Carlos asked who would like to smoke it. Silence reigned. Finally, Julian raised a finger. I was dumbfounded, never having seen him smoke anything before. He allowed the farmer to warm the cigar with a match and then give him a light while he puffed away, nodding as if he were a connoisseur. Our fellow day-trippers clapped.

"Julian, I didn't know you smoked cigars," I whispered, when we were seated back in the bus.

"No, no, I don't – not now – but I used to smoke them sometimes, when I was a young teacher in the mountains. You know, there was nothing else to do. But I am not used. Didn't you notice? I almost fainted after four inhalations." I was glad I hadn't noticed, because I enjoyed the sight of our fellow passengers admiring "my Cuban" as he savored his freshly rolled cigar.

———————

"Could I just ask you something?" It was the Canadian woman who had quizzed me at the beginning of the day. "Are you guys going on any other tours this week?"

"Nope, this is the only one," I answered. "We'll probably just stay in Havana after this. There's a lot Julian wants me to see – museums, concerts and plays."

"That's too bad," she said. "My husband and I really loved the way your friend explained Cuban schools. We'd do a tour with him anytime."

"Well, he's an expert," I said. "He was a school inspector for over twenty years and then a professor of English for another twenty."

"Oh, wow. You're so lucky," she twinkled.

"Yeah, I know."

———————

It was a long trip home in our ailing vehicle: we had to stop three more times while the poor driver dashed off into the evening gloom to get water for the radiator. And as if that was not enough of a trial for him, there were the usual bikes and horse-carts traveling on the side of the highway without any kind of light at all, as well as dilapidated trucks pretending to be buses, their backs full of passengers happily chatting to one another.

When I got back to Magdalena's after nine o'clock that evening, she was sitting in front of the blaring TV, sound asleep. Since I didn't want to be disturbed by another late-night bed-check, I coughed loudly and woke her. She took a minute to look around and turn down the volume before finding me in the gloom.

"*Buenas tardes*," I said. "I'm back."

"So late?" she said, trying to bring her watch into focus. "What happened?"

"Well, our bus had some problems with the radiator," I explained, "so we had to stop many times for repairs."

"The bus – I knew it!" she commented. "It's always the same."

As I lay in bed waiting for sleep, I realized that, despite the still unreliable transportation, Cuba wasn't really "always the same". In fact, it had changed in any number of ways since my last visit. Revised regulations allowing Cubans to start small businesses had already borne fruit. In only two years a bakery, a grocery and a pet shop had sprung up in the one small area of Havana we were familiar with. New restaurants had popped up, too. What was generally noticeable was that quality was rising – as well as prices. And to top it all, Julian had, before my very eyes, been offered a part-time job in the private sector. As Magdalena had noted, there were still massive problems with transport, but now with all this change going on, there was at least hope of better times to come.

15
THOSE WHO LEAVE AND THOSE WHO STAY

AGRANDDAUGHTER OF MAGDALENA'S WAS SITTING with us at the breakfast table. Not the one who spends the afternoon in Magdalena's apartment, but Yudilen, who was visiting from eastern Cuba.

Yudilen's name exemplifies a rather curious practice in Cuban name-giving: first names beginning with the letter Y. I noticed the phenomenon at the English teachers' conference the first time I was in Havana. There, younger teachers of both sexes surprised me with first names like Yuniesky, Yoenis, Yadinnis, Yilka and Yossenti. Their parents had followed Fidel Castro's advice not to give children traditional saints' names anymore, but to create a unique name for each child, starting with the letter Y. The made-up names were difficult for me to remember, but their owners seemed proud of them.

Magdalena's granddaughter, Yudilen, was pretty in a feminine way. Her shoulder-length fair hair and clear complexion made her look younger and more innocent than her twenty-seven years, although she did turn out to

186

be rather naïve. She was in Havana for an interview at the Canadian Embassy, to see if she qualified for a Canadian immigration visa.

She was in a kind of Catch-22 situation. As far as the Cuban government was concerned, she was free to leave Cuba. This marked a dramatic reversal in government policy, after years of persecuting anybody who so much as mentioned wanting to leave. She still had a year to go before completing her psychology degree. Financially speaking, it would be better to emigrate now, because if she finished her degree in Cuba, she would have to repay the total amount of her tuition in order to get permission to leave. This, in my opinion, was justified, as she was proposing to take her skills, which the Cuban government had paid for, to another country. However, now, without a degree, she was unqualified to work in Canada as a psychologist and would therefore not be accepted by the Canadians. She had already had the interview and was not optimistic about the outcome.

"I don't think they will take me," she admitted in a low voice, when Julian asked how the interview had gone.

"They are stupid if they don't take you, a clever girl like you. Look how long you've studied," said Magdalena, whose grandchildren were all the brightest and most beautiful in Cuba.

"Yes, but it's clear they won't accept her if she hasn't got a professional qualification," countered Julian.

"Why not? She can finish her studies in Canada in a year – or six months if she has to," insisted Magdalena.

"The woman said I had to learn much more English, or else French," muttered Yudilen, picking at her plastic-flower bracelet.

"Of course you do, of course you do. English is the key to the future," declared Julian in a professorial voice. This was one of his firm beliefs and he wasn't going to let the topic go by without an endorsement. "How can you expect the Canadians to accept you for work as a psychologist if your English is weak? You must take more courses as soon as you can. Intensive courses – that's what you need. Who are the English professors at your university?" Yudilen had to admit she didn't know and hadn't been near an English class for several years.

The conversation took an altogether different tack when Magdalena turned to me, still calling me Esther in 2011: "Esther – you're from Canada. Don't you know someone who can get her a visa? Can't you help her?"

I studied her face; she was serious. "Me? I'm very sorry, Magdalena, but I don't know anyone in the government." We let it drop there.

***

For those intent on leaving Cuba there are of course other strategies that can be followed. Among the most popular is finding a tourist girlfriend or boyfriend from a prosperous country like Canada or Spain, Switzerland or Chile and marrying them. I'd seen a good number of such Swiss-Cuban couples at the Cuban consulate in Bern when I collected my tourist visa. Yudilen didn't seem like the type of person who would opt for the marriage route, but you never know.

Even if a tourist relationship doesn't last long

enough for an exit visa, some Cubans are just happy to share a tourist's lifestyle for a day or two. I couldn't help noticing one of these lifestyle couples while Julian and I were having supper in a three-star hotel in Vedado. Just outside the restaurant door, in the hotel lobby, there was a small internet corner, with one or two decrepit computers provided for guests. Seated at one of them, her face about ten inches from the screen, was a young East-Asian woman – Korean or Chinese – alternately typing and searching the internet, apparently intent on getting information for the next leg of her trip. She didn't look especially rich or pretty – just computer-savvy and preoccupied. Kneeling on the floor beside her chair was a gorgeous young Afro-Cuban man, dressed in a green satin basketball uniform. He was definitely not focusing on the computer; his full attention was on the girl. In fact, he was trying to show her how much he cared for her by kissing her on the very arm with which she was busy typing. And he was not dispensing single kisses either, but planting a long row of kisses up and down that arm. The girl kept typing and studiously ignoring her would-be *amigo*, while he kept kissing and murmuring sweet nothings. The hotel waiter maintained a discreet distance, so it was up to the girl to extricate herself from the situation. Their "relationship" had probably started with an innocent conversation while she was sightseeing in the old town. I wondered how it would end; unfortunately we didn't stay long enough to find out.

I had heard about *jineteros*, or tourist hustlers, long before setting foot in Cuba. A good friend had told me that her Swiss husband was terrorized by one – in this case a female, a *jinetera* – during a stopover in Havana on his way to Nicaragua. While strolling along the Malecon in a Hawaii-shirt, enjoying the sea air and admiring the view, this Swiss businessman was accosted by a pretty young woman in jeans, who chatted him up. At first he was flattered. They walked and talked for a while. Then they sat down together on the sea wall, where she neatly entwined her arm in his, thereafter maintaining a vice-like hold. The poor Swiss was unable to avoid her other hand either, and became so panicky that, when he finally did manage to liberate his middle-aged body from her attentions, could only race back to his hotel – the Nacional, of course – and stay there for twenty-four hours until it was time to take a taxi to the airport.

Julian and I talked about many Cubans' wish to leave, too. Early one Sunday morning, just as the sun was illuminating more and more of the FOCSA Building, we met outside Magdalena's to walk the Malecon together before it got too hot, and before there were any other people. We strolled westwards along the seafront, away from the city center. To our right was the waist-high sea-wall running on and on into the distance. The sky was bright blue and cloudless and there was no one else around – only gulls, and the odd 1960s Plymouth, cruising the roads.

"So Florida's somewhere out there beyond the horizon, is it?" I said.

"Yes, unfortunately too close. It has encouraged too many people to risk their lives trying to escape." Julian shook his head.

"Did you ever think of leaving Cuba when you were younger?"

"Heh heh, no – not seriously. I was always more or less happy here. I always had a good and an interesting job. When I was in Mexico for three months one summer, giving a teacher training course, I thought a lot about how Isabel might come and join me and I could find a job there and then we would stay there, but it was just a daydream. I couldn't abandon my mother and my son. I couldn't stand it, never to see them again."

"No, you certainly couldn't leave your family. And with your job at the university – you're almost too respectable to leave."

"Well,... maybe. That's an interesting idea. It would be a scandal if a professor like me disappeared, but, you know... there were some very respected people who took advantage of a visit to the US or Spain to just stay there. They never came back. Even some of the Castro family – they live in the US and the Dominican Republic."

We walked on; the sun was beginning to scorch our backs. The Malecon made two ninety-degree turns, creating a half-hidden corner balcony over the water. Julian stopped dead and stared at the ground. The sidewalk was littered with used condoms, broken glass and a few unidentifiable but almost certainly unsavory objects. Julian took a deep breath.

"Now, here you see a really bad side of life in Cuba. Prostitution is illegal, and the police are trying to stop it, but that pushes it to places like this. Can you imagine? Can you *imagine*? Here in front of the Plaza de la Revolucion!"

At that point I didn't really care to imagine anything –

especially not the scene here last night, when the condoms were in use.

"Oh please don't worry, Julian," I said, "It's OK. Really. I'm not shocked. It's getting too hot anyway. Let's turn around and go back." So we about-faced into the sun and started our sweaty trudge back to Magdalena's.

"But it's a big medical problem – AIDS." Julian insisted. "I have been to Havana several times to represent Santa Clara at meetings on the AIDS problem. Many ordinary Cuban people don't know even the basic facts about AIDS – they are too embarrassed. And then it can happen that they are confronted with the problem in their own family because of situations like what we just saw here on the Malecon."

"Are they doing that so that they can leave Cuba?" I asked in all innocence.

"No, no. They are doing it to get money – for their family, for drugs… Well, maybe some are trying to get a foreign husband in that way, but not many."

The more I thought about Yudilen's situation, the sadder I felt about her wish to leave Cuba. How could she possibly cope with life in a new country with a different education system and a new language? She seemed barely prepared for life in Cuba. Did she really want to live apart from her Cuban family, or was this something her parents wanted for her, to have a life with more comfort and security? I couldn't tell, but doubted emigration was a good idea. As for Magdalena, it must have been inexpressibly painful for her to push her own granddaughter to leave the country, knowing that they might never see each other again.

Julian and I were on our way to visit the headquarters of Eusebio Leal, city historian of Havana and rescuer of its most beautiful buildings. In addition to being an architect and historian, Leal had devised a way to use tourist dollars to fund the preservation of old buildings, making the city more attractive to visitors. After some successful smaller restoration projects in the 1970s, Leal won Castro's support, and developed a master plan to renovate buildings in Habana Vieja, hiring dozens of architects, archaeologists, craftsmen and laborers.

In the "special period" of the 1990s, after the breakup of the Soviet Union, when Cuba's economy was hit by the loss of all material support from the Communist bloc, Castro realized he needed to promote tourism as Cuba's main source of income, so he asked Leal if he could come up with a way to save Havana without government funding. Leal proposed that his office be given *carte blanche* to generate its own revenue, using the income from tourism in the old town of Havana. Castro agreed and gave Leal seed money of $1 million, which was used to renovate three restaurants and the gorgeous Ambos Mundos hotel, where Hemingway is supposed to have written For Whom The Bell Tolls. Since then, Leal's operation has extended to sixteen hotels, a tour company, restaurants, museums and more, generating profits of over $20 million. Leal reinvests half the profits in new preservation work and half in social projects, such as health clinics, schools and senior centers in the old city. A member of the Socialist Party Central Committee, but also a Christian, he believes that the way to attract tourists is not with a Havana à la Disney, but with a Havana where real Cubans work and live – in real neighborhoods with local schools and hospitals. It certainly attracted me.

Julian and I turned the corner into Calle Cuba, on our way to the restored convent where Leal had his office. Typically, we had not been able to find out, either by phoning or by checking the newspaper, whether it was going to be open when we got there. Miraculously it was, and again, miraculously, we were the only tourists. From the street, one has no idea that a two-block-long oasis of greenest garden lies behind the rather plain and slightly neglected façade of the Convento de Santa Clara de Asis. An old man was sitting at a dusty table inside the door, chatting with two of his friends. He took a CUC from each of us by way of admission fee, offering no ticket in return.

We entered the vast inner cloister area, which we had all to ourselves as we wandered around the central garden, gazing up into the tall palms and eucalyptus, peering through flourishing vines and hedges until we came to a fountain with a statue of a nymph at its center. Sitting down on the rim, we contemplated the harmony and grace of the cloister buildings.

"This is so lovely, Julian. I never thought there was anything like this in Havana. It's so restful and... and lush."

"Yes, I am surprised too. And nobody here! We have found our own oasis."

"Can you smell something spicy and sweet? I think it must be those big orange flowers on the vine hanging from that eucalyptus. What is that?"

"Sorry, I have no idea. Heather, you should know by now that I am shamefully ignorant about botany."

"And the buildings surrounding the garden – they've all been perfectly restored. The paint is new."

"Well, of course, that is our friend Eusebio Leal's work. I've read that part of this convent is a hostel for tourists now."

The garden was surrounded by a tall cloister of stone arches, by galleries of classical columns casting eye-pleasing patterns of light and shade, graceful stone stairways leading to rooms for nuns and pilgrims – maybe for workers, too. Julian and I continued our walk through the lower galleries and garden paths, listening out for the voices of Leal and his team. All we heard were those of the men at the front door, now sounding as if they were playing dominoes, and of two cleaning ladies who were taking a break in a small central pavilion. We slowly gravitated to this area, which turned out to be a very simple snack bar. To our disappointment, we were told that no snacks were available, as the person responsible had not shown up for work.

"But there are certainly cold drinks in that fridge, aren't there?" Julian pressed them.

"*Si, es possible,*" they agreed, as they went on nonchalantly smoking.

"Well... if we were to give you the money, could you give us two bottles of juice or cola from the fridge? We're very thirsty because it's so hot." Julian suggested with extreme politeness. Without a word, one of them got up, opened the fridge, removed two bottles of cola and put them on our table. Julian handed her two CUCs without a word. I don't normally drink cola but this one tasted exquisite.

"And Eusebio Leal?" continued Julian, without missing a beat. "Is he here today?"

"No, no. He's not here," they replied in unison. "He's out working."

So we drained our bottles and returned to the cloister garden to admire the fruits of Eusebio's labor in his absence, appreciating the subtlety of the colors he'd chosen and the potted plants accentuating the rhythm of the arches. It would have to suffice that we'd been one handshake away from the great man himself.

Later that same day Julian and I went to an operetta called *Cecilia Valdés*. "Here, it's the most popular *zarzuela* of all," Julian explained, "because it takes place in Cuba in colonial times. It's about a mulatta – a woman of ehm mixed race – whose name is Cecilia Valdes. Her father is a white plantation owner, and she is his illegitimate daughter but she doesn't know this. Unfortunately, Cecilia falls in love with her father's son – so, in other words, she falls in love with her white half-brother. And she becomes pregnant. Very complex, in a psychological way."

"Wow," I remarked, "pretty heavy social and ethical problems. So what happens?"

"Well, there's a black slave who loves Cecilia, too, and when she is abandoned by her half-brother, this slave kills him to avenge Cecilia. Both of them, Cecilia and the black man, are punished. It's very tragic."

"Hmm. Really complicated. So there are white, mixed

race and black characters in this operetta. And love, sex and incest, illegitimacy and murder and revenge and prison..."

"Heh, heh. Yes, and singing and dancing, too. Do you want to see it?"

"You bet I do. It sounds a little like an American musical called Showboat."

Entering Havana's Gran Teatro felt like a trip back to the 19th century. Seats, carpet and curtain were in dark red velvet, but of course much faded, as it probably hadn't been refurbished in fifty years. What was newer was the air-conditioning. And of course the audience was perfectly attuned to the bourgeois entertainment that *zarzuela* represents. It was an overwhelmingly white audience, consisting of family groups represented by three generations, with the children as young as eight or nine. Then there were groups of older women in shawls, fluttering fans as they chatted, which was totally unnecessary in view of the air conditioning. Everyone was dressed in their best clothes, including the children, who were busy chasing each other in the aisles.

When the curtain finally rose, I was surprised that there were no musicians in the pit – only an offstage recording of an orchestra playing the music. But the audience loved the *zarzuela*, even though – or perhaps because – they had heard it several times before. The story was poignant, the music sweet, the singing true, the acting overdone, the dancing enthusiastic. The audience cried and applauded. They loved this remnant from the 19th century, from the good old, bad old days long before the revolution. These were Cubans who had stayed, I told myself, people who had not jumped onto boats and planes headed for Miami. They may have lost their wealth, but they still had their cultural preferences, perhaps a few privileges and their sense of belonging in Cuba. Somehow – although it must have been difficult – these members of the old bourgeoisie had come to terms with Castro's new socialist Cuba and found a niche for themselves, and a *raison d'être*. Culture and patriotism appeared to play a role in this self-understanding. Like Eusebio Leal, the musician Zenaida Romeu, the ballerina Alicia Alonso, my good friend Julian, and many more of the eleven million Cubans who had decided to stay and pursue their professional goals, love of country and love of Cuban culture went hand in hand.

16
CUBAN HEROES

THERE ARE NO STATUES OF the Castro brothers to be seen in Cuba. Once in a while, along the highway, Fidel's silhouette may appear on a billboard, accompanied by the slogan '*Comandante en Jefe, ordene*' (Commander-in-Chief, give me my orders!), but otherwise his likeness is surprisingly scarce. Che Guevara ranks higher in the Cuban pantheon, but there are not many Che statues to be seen either, although his Christ-like portrait is painted on many walls and billboards around the country. No, in terms of statue population, it is José Marti who is the absolute hero-in-chief of Cuba, with at least one statue or bust in every town and village. Unfortunately, few English speakers have ever heard of Marti, although he was a gifted poet and prolific writer, a patriot and a fearless leader of men, who sacrificed his life and happiness in the struggle for Cuban independence.

On the first page of the Marti biography that he'd sent to me by way of Nelson, Julian had written:

Dear Heather,
Finally I was able to find this book in

English. I hope that by reading it, your life
may be enriched through the knowledge
of one of the most extraordinary human
beings that has ever lived – our beloved
hero José Marti.

Thus I was not too surprised when Julian suggested
visiting Marti's childhood home.

"Heather," he started, "what do you think if we make a
pilgrimage to the place where José Marti was born?"

"Sounds like a good idea to me," I said. "I'd love to
see it." This was actually a slight exaggeration of my
enthusiasm. I was feeling hugely guilty about not finishing
the Marti biography, which had turned out to be poorly
translated and embarrassing in its adulatory language.

"We could take a *bicitaxi* to go there – it's cheaper
than a taxi and good for short distances," suggested Julian.

"Oh boy. You know I've been wanting to ride in
a *bicitaxi* since my first day here." Julian knew how to
motivate me – I had a pronounced weakness for the more
original forms of Cuban transport.

So Julian hailed a *bicitaxi*, a sort of low-tech rickshaw,
and told the driver we wanted to travel the few blocks to
the *Casa Natal de José Marti,* located at Leonor Perez 314.
Our driver was, like almost all *bicitaxistas*, dark-skinned
and wiry. He was lightly clad, but perspiring noticeably
when he offered his hand, as I stepped up onto a metal
stirrup and insinuated myself into the tiny space between
roof, back-rest and knee-banger. Julian was attempting to
do the same – minus the helping hand – on the other
side of the vehicle. The only way the passenger seat would

accommodate the two of us was for Julian to put his arm around me. And even with this minor adjustment, our outside knees and lower legs still protruded awkwardly. It was at that point that I realized why I had only ever seen a single person or a woman and her shopping being transported in a *bicitaxi*. The flat, sheet-metal roof was so low that Julian had to let his head loll sideways towards the arm that was encircling my shoulders. Passersby stopped to watch our slow progress, no doubt convinced that the kind *bicitaxista* was transporting two inebriated tourists back to their hotel.

A further discomfort factor was the lack of springs and inflated tires: *bicitaxis* make their passengers aware of every bump in the road. Motorized traffic whizzed around us, but we trundled along in the right lane, never missing a pothole. By the time Julian and I extricated ourselves from the vehicle fifteen minutes later, our driver was sweating even more copiously than before. The road had been flat and our speed slow, but Julian and I together must have weighed at least 140 kilos. The fare was two CUCs; Julian gave the driver a well-deserved three.

José Marti's two-story home, set in a quiet city street, resembled a child's playhouse. It was in perfect condition, freshly painted in bright blue and yellow. We'd entered and were climbing the fragile staircase when Julian said, "Heather, tell me: which part of José Marti's life did you like best?"

I gulped; the moment of truth had arrived. Owing to the abbreviated time I'd spent reading the biography, I had no choice but to recall something from Marti's early years. "Well," I replied, desperately wracking my brains to remember something worthy, "I was very touched by the time when Marti was imprisoned as a teenager – when he shared the little bit of money his mother had given him with his fellow prisoners."

"Ah yes, yes, I remember," said Julian, "his parents gave him money for coffee and he gave it to other prisoners."

When we got to the top, we were met by a female guard, who was obviously there to make sure nothing went missing and to answer questions. Since Julian and I were alone in the house, we asked many.

"So is this really the inkwell of our national apostle?" was the sort of thing Julian wanted to know.

"*Bueno*," said the guard, obviously on top of her stuff, "This is Marti's house of birth. He was only three years old when his parents left this house, so he did not use that inkwell *here*, but it was given to the museum by descendants of Marti's landlord from the house where he lived when he was attending the teachers' seminary in Havana."

"*Ah si, si. Claro.*" said Julian, satisfied with this explanation. The upstairs rooms that the family had actually inhabited were sparsely furnished with several plain chairs and a table, a child's cradle and a few bookcases.

"Ask her about that braid of Marti's hair in the glass case," I suggested. "Why is it so blond? Marti had dark hair, didn't he?"

Julian laughed and translated the question for me, to which the guard replied in Spanish, "Marti's family were all fair-skinned. His six sisters were also blond as children, as you can see in some of the family photographs downstairs. Unfortunately most of them died before their mother, some very young."

We took our time going through the photos and documents, but the impression that remained with me was of cramped rooms that must have held rather small people spending their days within a few feet of each other. Behind the house, though, there was a little courtyard with palms and ferns and shady nooks, which I could imagine made a wonderful place for children to play in.

The ground floor rooms, which had not been inhabited by the Martis, displayed official documents, photographs and private diaries, with Marti's high forehead making him easy to pick out in any picture. What impressed me most was that Marti lived in exile in New York from 1881 to 1895, where he published articles, wrote beautiful poetry and translated books from and into English, French and Spanish. What must it have been like for him to write articles and poems for readers in all of Latin America, to represent various Latin American governments in New York, but not be able to return to Cuba? Perhaps worst of all for him was that his wife and young son were living in Mexico. When Marti finally ended his exile and secretly returned to the mountains of eastern Cuba to join the battle for independence – a model for Fidel Castro and his band sixty years later – he was killed within five weeks of his return.

It was very special being virtually alone with Julian in this house that had produced the greatest hero in the struggle for Cuban independence. For Julian, walking through the tiny house was as inspiring as visiting

Abraham Lincoln's log cabin would be for an American. I'd had my doubts when Julian suggested it, since I mistakenly thought I would be seeing another poorly maintained Cuban museum. But now, after studying the photographs and hearing more about Marti's life – and above all appreciating how much Marti meant to both the guard and Julian – I was so glad I'd come.

———— ••• ————

At the end of my first visit in 2008, Julian and I had talked about crossing Havana harbor to see the fortresses on the other side, so in 2011, when Julian asked what I wanted to do during our time together in Havana, I said, "Well, one thing I'd like to do is cross Havana harbor. I don't know how… do we take a ferry or what?"

"Oh, of course – we can do that," said Julian. "Yes, there's a ferry to Regla."

"Regla?" I repeated, since I'd never heard of the place before. "Is that the name of the fortress?"

Magdalena, who was making coffee for our breakfast, joined in at this point. "Regla?" she said, "You're going to Regla? *Que bueno!*"

And so that is how my request for a cross-harbor jaunt to a fortress came to be misinterpreted as a desire to visit the votive church at Regla, which is just across Havana harbor from the old town. Magdalena now became quite animated, explaining that she had made a vow to visit the Regla church annually and leave flowers on the altar, and that we could now carry out the promise on her behalf, since she couldn't do it anymore. After seeing how pleased she was, I couldn't possibly ask to change plans.

On the day of our Regla trip, Julian and I bustled through the old town, full of purpose and energy. Most other people were not walking fast – or not walking at all in some cases. It was hot, and most of them were either standing in queues outside the telephone office or the pharmacy, sitting on stools at street-side pizza bars, or waiting for children to be released from school. We marched past them all and made our way to Cespedes, heading for the empty cruiser docks. As we moved down that street, I felt a swoon of nostalgia at the sight of the old Packards and Studebakers, Pontiacs and Nashes parked there. Finally we found the narrow alleyway leading to the Regla ferry. It was already full, with twenty to thirty would-be passengers already standing in a massed queue – the lucky ones in the shade and the less lucky ones in the broiling sun – waiting with their tickets at hand. Julian assured me that there would be enough room for everybody when the ferry turned up.

The sturdy little vessel chugged up to the dock in about ten minutes. When given the signal, our fellow queue-mates moved as one onto the tiny ferry, Julian and myself swept along with them like two pebbles in a lava flow. The ferry was the size of a tugboat – in fact, it probably was a re-purposed tugboat – and consisted of a large inner standing room without benches and just a few metal poles to hold on to. The room was packed.

The voyage across the harbor afforded a better view of my fellow pilgrims. They were not well-to-do. One or two men had old bicycles with them, but most of the passengers were females between the ages of twenty and eighty, black and white and in-between, many wearing revealing tank tops and skin-tight Lycra shorts, and carrying ostentatious bouquets of white flowers, mostly artificial. Havana harbor, which was as smooth as a lake, reflected the light blue sky – except that it also featured swirling rainbow streamers of oil. The ferry was covered with black grime and smelled like a car repair pit.

When we'd drawn within two hundred yards of the Regla shore, a sudden rustling arose from the lightly clad female passengers, who were starting to prepare themselves for their encounter with the Blessed Virgin of Regla. Cotton skirts and shawls were whipped out of plastic bags to cover bare legs and shoulders, and loose manes were tied back chastely, as a general air of reverent expectancy descended on the pilgrims.

Upon docking, most passengers rushed off the boat as they had rushed on. Julian and I stepped aside and waited till they'd all debarked, then followed up the short path to the *Iglesia de Nuestra Senora de Regla*, an unspectacular creamy-white 19th century church. As promised, Julian bought a small bouquet of freesia for Magdalena from a flower seller just outside the door. He also bought votive candles to take home to his wife, who is a practicing Catholic.

When we entered the church, Julian and I split up. I wandered around the nave, enjoying the religious music floating down from several high loudspeakers. Statues of more than a dozen saints were displayed in small wall-alcoves situated on both sides of the fairly large room. I went from saint to saint, reading about their origins and powers. As I gazed around the church, now echoing with recorded Gregorian chants, my eyes fell upon many of the people who had been with us on the ferry. Old and young alike, they were kneeling before the alcoves, lighting candles, arranging flowers, saying a rosary, praying, or just sitting in a pew, their faces hidden in their hands. The prevalent emotion had changed from bustling gaiety to intense concentration.

While I was making those observations, Julian had sought out the altar of the Virgin of Regla, which is in a larger side chapel. He was kneeling on the step before the altar after offering his candle and Magdalena's flowers. I admired his ability to take on the mission with so much empathy. The statue on the altar was a standing black Madonna, dressed in copious satin robes of white and light-blue, crowned, and holding the infant Jesus, who – strangely enough – was pink-fleshed. Behind her was a naive painting of the port of Havana filled with sailboats.

The Madonna of Regla is of course venerated in the Cuban Catholic Church, but what I hadn't realized is that she is also associated with Santeria, the Afro-Cuban religion, where she is worshipped as Yemaya, the spirit of the ocean and moon and the patron of sailors. According to legend, the black statue in the Regla church was carved by or for St Augustine "The African" in the 5th century, and later brought to Spain and then to Cuba. More recently, Cubans escaping to US shores by boat or raft have also claimed the protection of the Black Virgin of Regla.

The church is quite definitely Catholic, but it was interesting to note the strong roots of African religion in Cuba, where West African slaves, mostly of Yoruba ethnicity, were forced to take on their Spanish masters' religion, with the result that the original Yoruba gods or spirits – called *orishas* – became identified with Catholic saints, so that by praying to a particular Catholic saint, the slaves also felt they were praying to a particular *orisha*. Today it is relatively common to see Cubans, especially dark-skinned women, dressed completely in white. During my first visit to Cuba, I'd noticed women wearing white clothes, turbans, shoes and gloves and carrying white parasols, and asked Julian who they were.

"Oh those are people who are hoping to become priests in the religion called Santeria. It's a local religion that combines Catholic and African beliefs and saints," he answered.

"But why are they wearing white? Is it some kind of uniform?"

"No, no. White signifies that they are purifying themselves to become priests. It is a long process I think, but I must admit I am a bit ignorant about it."

"Is it like voodoo?"

"No, no, it's based on Catholic saints, so it's not like voodoo."

After a while Julian and I left the church and found a place to sit on the low retaining wall that overlooked the harbor. Across the mirror of water, old Havana presented itself as a hazy row of pastel buildings.

"Hey, look at that!" I said, "Havana looks gorgeous from here – and the colors are even better reflected in the silver water."

"Mhm, mhm," Julian acknowledged my comment, not looking up.

I waited a minute and then asked softly: "What are you thinking about, *amigo*? The church?"

"Not really the church, no. I am just glad we could do this for Magdalena. It was really important to her because she isn't able to make the pilgrimage herself anymore. I think perhaps she made a vow concerning her older daughter – you know, the one who died of lung cancer?"

"Yes, I'm glad we made the effort, too," I said. "I didn't really want to come here when we started out this morning. I didn't think it would show me anything I'd be interested in, but I was wrong. I'm sure it showed me a lot more than visiting the forts."

The day had shed a new light on Cuban society for me, especially on the space where white– and Afro-Cubans come together to share religions and values. The people on our ferry had held intense religious beliefs, and were serious about the purpose of their visit to the Black Madonna of Regla. In walking round the church I witnessed the fact that Yoruba *orishas* had come to cohabit with Catholic saints, and that both were being worshipped and prayed to in the same way. It was interesting, too, to note that white Cubans have begun to practice the rituals of Santeria, as if they thirst for a vibrant, emotional form of religion after sixty years of sober political ritual. I was reminded of the women I'd seen at the grave of La Milagrosa in the big cemetery in Havana. They, too, seemed to need ritual and emotional belief in their lives. The official party line might still be that religion was the opium of the people, but I'd experienced vivid proof of its resurgence in Cuba.

Straight after our Regla pilgrimage we returned to

Magdalena's kitchen to report our mission accomplished. She was sitting in a dim corner with a basket of Cuban garlic in her lap, peeling the tiny cloves with a sharp knife without looking, performing the chore by touch alone.

"Many people in the church?" she asked.

"Quite a few," said Julian, "but enough room for everybody. I got your flowers – freesias – and placed them in a big vase in front of the *Virgen*."

"*Todo bien. Gracias, gracias*," she thanked him.

"Ehm Magdalena, I wanted to ask you, was the vow about your daughter – the one who had cancer?" inquired Julian delicately.

Our hostess did not answer but put her basket on the table, got up from her stool and left the room.

We looked at each other, wondering if we had said the wrong thing. "I didn't think it would make her leave," whispered Julian. "Maybe you could have a look to see where she is?"

At that moment we could hear Magdalena's flip-flops returning from her bedroom. She had three black and white photos in her hand, which she tossed onto the table. The top one was of herself as a young woman with a heart-shaped face. I recognized her immediately, although I wouldn't have guessed how pretty she'd once been. She had blond highlights in her hair and was wearing a sundress, apparently sitting at a nightclub table and smiling sweetly into the camera lens. "*Que linda*!" she commented, "I was nineteen – my husband took it." She had once been very pretty indeed.

The second photo was of her eldest daughter, who must have been in her twenties when the picture was taken. She had, in Magdalena's opinion, made the mistake of getting mixed up with the Castros. Her daughter had married the son of Fidel and Raul's brother, Ramon – or Mongo, as Magdalena called him. The wedding was a nightmare for her as the mother of the bride. She wanted Paula to wear something pretty, but by that time there was not even any decent cloth available in Cuba, let alone a wedding dress. In the end they had to take the satin lining out of her husband's old suits to make the dress – a neighbor had helped her. And when they went to the wedding, dressed in hand-me-down and made-over clothes, they noticed that Raul's daughters were all wearing beautiful new dresses – probably imported from Spain. And then, after all that trouble, the marriage was over within a few years. Her son-in-law was totally spoiled and unstable and was always having run-ins with the law. He finally emigrated to the Dominican Republic and Paula came home again and smoked her way to an early death.

"When she was diagnosed with cancer I made a vow to go to Regla every year. But it didn't help… Still, a vow is a vow, so thank you for going. May God reward you."

"And what about your husband?" asked Julian. "Was he affected by your daughter's death?"

"No, no, he was already dead. I met him when I was 18," she said. "He was working for Cuban radio – very successful, a good journalist.. That's why we lived here in this apartment – it's near the radio studios."

"*Ah si, si,*" confirmed Julian, "the studio's very near here."

"*Bueno.* We started a family – a boy, a girl. Then came the revolution in 1959 and Cuban radio was turned into

Radio Rebelde. A few people at the radio had been pro-Batista; they were thrown out – just gone or put in prison, I don't know. But my husband wasn't pro-Batista. No, he just wanted to go on as a journalist, just doing a good job... Here's a picture of him at work."

We gazed at the third photograph, which showed a profile view of a serious, bespectacled man in his early forties, reading a text into a studio microphone as he sat at a desk. He looked business-like and professional.

"But he couldn't work the way he wanted to. Those young revolutionaries with no journalistic training – none! absolutely none! – they were given jobs as his co-workers, and even as his bosses. They didn't know what they were doing. He tried to continue, to go on doing a good job, but that's when he started losing his voice. At first it was hoarse – like a cold – and then after several months it became a whisper. Two years after the revolution he was forced to resign from the radio because he lost his voice completely."

Julian and I sat staring at the photo on the table. I raised my eyes to Magdalena. She wasn't crying, but her eyes were moist.

The result was a deep depression from which her husband never recovered. He stopped talking altogether, took to his bed and finally wouldn't even get up to use the toilet. Magdalena kept him at home for as long as possible, feeding and cleaning him like a baby, getting a neighbor to help her lift him, but in the end she had to have him institutionalized.

"*Era terrible, terrible, terrible!*" She cupped her stubby hands to her temples.

"And the children?" I asked.

"Two were already in school, learning about the heroes of the revolution, and I was looking after the baby at home. I couldn't even go with him in the ambulance."

I shook my head, at a loss for words.

"He died there in the mental hospital. He never said another word to me."

It occurred to me that revolutions must have many unintended victims like Magdalena's husband – people who, above all, want to go on as before, just doing a good job. For Magdalena, the revolution had been a disaster. She had lost almost everything: her childhood home, her husband, all comforts. Yet somehow she had had the strength of character to care for her husband during his terrible depression and raise three children alone, holding on to the apartment through decades of belt-tightening and deprivation. When I thought of everything she'd been through and how she still had the mental strength to protest and support her family, she seemed heroic.

17
SANTA CLARA AT LAST

I T'S MARCH 2013, AND TWO years have passed
since my last visit to Cuba. But this time I'm not
in Havana; this time Julian has invited me to his
hometown of Santa Clara, from where we can make day
trips by car to places in central Cuba. It works out very
well, travel-wise, because there are now direct charter
flights from Halifax to Santa Clara airport, which means
it only takes four hours to get from where my parents live
to where Julian lives – an easy hop for me in the middle
of a family visit.

Bubbling with happy anticipation, I approach the
simple Arrivals terminal of Santa Clara Airport. I'm
looking forward to seeing Julian again, to meeting his
family and just to spending another vacation in Cuba,
with its balmy temperatures and interesting people. The
short charter flight was fine. For some reason I got a
seat in the front row, and, as a result, was first down the
gangway steps and onto the tarmac. Now I'm leading a
long line of stiff and sleepy tourists, their arms full of
neck-pillows, Gameboys, duty-free bags and no-longer-
needed winter coats. It's 8 p.m. in Santa Clara and a warm

breeze signals that we're well and truly away from the snowbanks of the Maritimes.

I enter the terminal and see the same set-up as in Havana: a long row of booths with flimsy plywood doors. It's time to talk to the immigration officer again. I march up to one of the doors with a big smile on my face. I know the routine now. This time the officer is a tanned, clean-shaven young man in the usual short-sleeved khaki military uniform. He takes my passport and papers and inspects them carefully without smiling. Because he doesn't see the charter operator's stamp on my visa, he asks if I am staying at a beach resort like the other Canadians on my flight. No, I say truthfully, I'm staying in Santa Clara. "*Donde*?" he asks, switching to Spanish. I say I don't know exactly where, but I'm visiting a friend, and the friend knows where. What am I going to do in Santa Clara, he wants to know. My mind goes blank; my Spanish dissolves. I hear myself babbling: "Oh I'm a tourist… and we uh visit churches and… and uh see things." Overcome by suddenly having to explain my purpose in Spanish, I grasp at any straw of vocabulary I can remember. He calls another officer. I glance through the booth's open door; my fellow passengers are lined up ten to a queue outside.

The second officer asks me in English why I am here. I manage to blurt out that I am here to visit a friend, that we are colleagues, we do the same work, and that I am visiting him and his family here.

"You go to churches." he states accusingly.

"Well, yes, but not only – as a tourist," I say.

"Come with me please," he says, and steers me back

out of the booth, across the hall full of gaping Canadians and into a small, white-walled, windowless room at the side. We are followed by four more young Cubans in uniform. I get one of the two folding chairs; a young woman gets the other. She starts asking me, in slow and shaky English, my name, where I live, where I will stay in Cuba, what I plan to do here. The others stand and listen as if this is a lesson in English interrogation. And it *is* an interrogation: the overhead lights are extremely bright and the air in the room is getting thicker by the second. One of the other officers appears to be taking notes. I can feel my mouth going dry as rising fear hollows out my self-confidence. I keep trying to will up some saliva so I don't sound guilty of whatever it is they're worried about. I think it was the churches, dammit. Shouldn't have mentioned visiting churches. I only mentioned them because I know the Spanish word for church.

"Where do you living in Santa Clara?" the young woman wants to know.

I say I don't know the address, but it is a *hostal* near the center. My friend will take me there, he is waiting outside. She asks for his name; I give it. There is a quick consultation in Spanish. The four standing officers leave and I am alone with the young woman who asked all the questions. I try to summon a smile. She smiles back.

"When you speaking English I can understand you very good," she says.

"I am an English teacher," I say by way of explanation. "Your English is good." I am regaining familiar ground now and trying to breathe normally again.

"No, no, is not good," she says modestly and smiles, pleased.

An officer re-enters our room carrying a small plastic card. It is Julian's Cuban ID. They examine it closely and copy the details into a form.

"Is OK. Please...," she says and opens the door. I am now free to enter Cuba.

I shoulder my daypack and am led from the interrogation room through customs. All other passengers have by now cleared immigration and are picking up their luggage from the customs hall. They regard me curiously. One woman from the plane approaches.

"Hey, what happened there? Are you OK?" she asks.

"Yup, fine," I try to answer breezily, though my knees are still jelly. "Just a misunderstanding because I'm not staying at a resort."

In reality, I feel like I'm emerging from a near-death experience.

My suitcase is standing among the last ones left for pick-up. I grab its good old handle, telescope it and stagger outdoors, feeling shaken and bruised and not nearly as enthusiastic about Cuba as I was half an hour earlier. I scan the crowd. There's Julian standing in the road in front of the airport building. I knew he was there because they got his ID, but I'm relieved to see him in the flesh. I walk over and hug him hard. He doesn't seem troubled in the slightest.

"So, Heather, welcome to Santa Clara!" he says in his jovial, teacher's voice. "Did you have a good flight?"

"Yes, great. But I thought I'd never get through immigration. They took me into a little room, you know?"

"Well, you are here now, among friends, and that is what matters," he smooths things over. "Ehm this is Ernesto. He will drive us back to Santa Clara."

I smile at the short, serious man standing next to Julian and shake his hand, still so shattered by my feelings in the interrogation room that I can't think of anything to say in Spanish. My nerves jangling, I get into the back seat of Ernesto's car and ride the ten dark kilometers back to town, trying to calm down enough to respond to Julian's conversation.

———————

Since my last visit in 2011, Julian and I now communicate most often by email. He's learned to use one of the two laptops I've given them for his emails. These are taken to the university on a flash drive and sent from his university email account by his son, who uses the other laptop every day in his translation work. Julian still feels that pen and paper letters are more private and less likely than emails to be screened by Cuban censors, but he likes the immediacy of emails, as do I.

As foreseen during my last visit, Julian has started teaching private English courses for adults four evenings a week, thus supplementing his retirement income. Although the level of English in the courses is not high, Julian spends considerable time preparing his lessons. The program is supported by Loyola University in Chicago, and they use American materials. Operating the computer, light projector and CD player in his new high-tech classroom sometimes stresses him, but he's basically happy to learn something new. Technology is not Julian's strong point, but he rises to an occasion with the best of them.

On the family side, Julian's ninety-seven-year-old mother is still alive and living in Julian's house, which is really her house. Amelia has suffered from senile dementia for several years now, which means that someone must always be at home to mind her. Sending a parent to a nursing home is almost unheard of in Cuba; a family member can usually be found to assume care-taking duties. This seems to be his wife Isabel's job most days, but she is often helped by Julian or their son, Gabriel. Lately, Amelia has started walking around for one or two hours at night, depriving Julian or his son of sleep.

The Presbyterian Church in Santa Clara has continued to participate in visiting programs with other Protestant churches, mainly from the US and Germany. Julian almost always acts as the Spanish-English interpreter, to facilitate these visits. He has also been asked to travel to the US more than once to represent the Cuban Presbyterian Church. However, no actual travel has come of the invitations, either because he has not received a visa or because he has withdrawn his application due to family or teaching commitments.

In many of his letters and emails over the last two years, Julian has referred to changes in the economic situation resulting from Raul Castro's new policies. He's mentioned changes like the 400,000 Cubans now employed in the private sector, one of whom – a former colleague from the university – now earns more money by driving tourists from Santa Clara airport to their hotels on the north coast. There is the expectation that some kind of rapprochement will be achieved between the US and Cuba, and that the economy will improve as a result. Jimmy Carter has visited and called for better relations. Pope Benedict XVI has visited and said mass for hundreds of thousands, the services being broadcast on Cuban state television. State control seems to be softening on a number of fronts.

Julian's son, Gabriel, has given up his full-time state work contract as a university English translator and has gone freelance, which is more lucrative. He and a business partner now get English-Spanish translating jobs via email from an agent in Columbia, who is taking advantage of their rock-bottom rates. People in Cuba still don't have internet access at home, but university email may be used if one is discreet.

To help connect my world with Julian's, I've given him a subscription to the Guardian Weekly, which he reads closely and with great interest, making lists of the articles he has read in its pages. Since I read the Guardian Weekly, too, we have something else in common and sometimes refer to specific articles in our correspondence.

Things have been happening in my life, too. Since seeing Julian in Havana in March 2011, I've launched myself into a number of new projects and directions. First of all, I've done some travelling – to the ruins of Pompeii and Herculaneum in Italy, and to the Greek island of Cos. Herculaneum and Pompeii were places I'd always wanted to visit since studying archeology at Harvard; Cos is an island that my flat-mate Helga and I have explored by bike and on foot many times. Besides traveling, I've taken a couple of year-long Open University courses: one, a

Latin course based on reading the Aeneid, and the other, a creative writing course, where I gathered the courage to write this book.

Among more ongoing projects, I've cycled respectable lengths of the rivers Danube and Elbe in Germany, and hiked up and down a number of not-too-challenging mountains in Switzerland. And to satisfy my permanent urge to improve the world, I've spent months campaigning and ultimately getting Swiss financial support for St. Martin's Girls Secondary School in Mbingu, Tanzania, which I hope to visit someday soon. In May 2012, we opened our household to a woolly, fourteen-year-old Tibetan terrier, who is a steady source of laughter and affection. I usually work on my Open University assignments with Cheerio curled up under my desk.

And, finally, my visits to Nova Scotia have increased to a rate of three or four times a year. This is because my father, who is now ninety-three, has started having regular medical crises related to kidney and heart failure.

While there have been changes in my life and Julian's, in Cuba and in the world, some things haven't changed at all. The scarcity of Cuban long-distance bus transportation has remained unchanged. Julian has solved it for my third visit by finding us Ernesto, a Santa Clara taxi driver. Ernesto has agreed to be our chauffeur for more or less the whole time I'm there. He'll take us on daily excursions to the places he and Julian have picked out for me to see: the northern keys, the Escambray mountains, Trinidad and so on. His estimated costs for fuel and his time are very reasonable: an average of $60 a day.

There's no way I can sleep at Julian's house, which is

fully occupied, with its five people and three bedrooms. Instead, Julian has found me a *hostal*, a bed and breakfast, which I now know is called *Hostal Casita*, where I can have my own room with bath for a very reasonable 25 CUCs a night. We pull up in front of a white row-house on a quiet Santa Clara street. As I extricate myself from the low back seat, Ernesto yanks my suitcase from the trunk and drags it up the high step into the front doorway. The proprietors, José and Teresita, are waiting just inside. After introductions, they show me to my room, which is at the back of the house, beyond a palm-filled atrium that is open to the stars. My room is high-ceilinged and equipped with a fridge, fan and TV. As in Magdalena's apartment in Havana, there is an en suite bathroom. The bedroom's high windows are, once again, glassless and louvered: I will sleep well with all the fresh air.

No time to look around longer though, because Ernesto is waiting to drive us to Julian's, where I'm to have dinner with the whole family. I've been curious about Julian's house and family for a long time, but it's now after nine p.m. and I'm tired and gradually unwinding from my encounter with Cuban border security at the airport. I brace myself for speaking Spanish with Julian's wife, Isabel, and his daughter-in-law, Marilys. And for eating dinner in the middle of the night.

The family are waiting in the living room of the single-story brown row-house, which opens directly onto sidewalk steps. I am handed round from person to person, kissing Isabel, Gabriel and Marilys twice on each cheek. It really is a pleasure to see and hear the voices of people I've heard so much about. Julian's wife leads me to the wooden rocking chair in a corner of the living room. She's much shorter than Julian and must have been extremely pretty at one time. She keeps her hair dark and short, and wears rouge and eye makeup. Their only son, Gabriel, is multi-tasking, pouring beers and speaking to me in excellent rapid-fire English as well as running to the kitchen, anxious to help in any way he can. His pretty wife, Marilys, who works as a librarian at the university, seems shy and overwhelmed by all the English; she quickly exits to the kitchen to get back to dinner preparations.

The cozy living room is packed with bookshelves, a TV, a desk and seating for at least six people. After a beer aperitif, we withdraw to the back kitchen, which this evening has been converted into a dining room. On our way to dinner, we walk through two small, darkened bedrooms – first Julian and Isabel's and then his mother's. A thin body is curled up asleep under a sheet. "That's my mother; she's gone to bed," Julian comments as he pilots me by the shoulders past her bed. There's no hall or corridor, so one simply walks through all the rooms to get to the back of the house. The next room is Isabel's kitchen, which is functioning as *the* kitchen this evening. Finally, there's Marilys's kitchen, which has been re-purposed as our dining room. It contains the two families' amalgamated kitchen tables, covered with a festive white sheet. I'm seated at the head of the table, while dishes are rushed in from the next room: salad, fried chicken, fried fish, yucca, rice and beans, green beans, fried plantain. They've gone all out with the menu and it smells delicious. I hope I can eat enough at this hour to do it justice. Isabel's little dog, Cynthia, makes her presence known by pressing her wet nose against my bare legs. She's smelled the chicken and speculates that I might be an easy touch.

Our conversation at the table is slow and slightly awkward, in both English and Spanish; first steps in getting to know each other. I remember to ask Julian if he wants to say grace. He does. Then we dig in. My plate's emptying and I'm a bit drunk after my second beer. It's easy for me to converse in English with the two men, but I must remember to say a few things in bad Spanish to include the women. I compliment them on the food and ask about the dog. Finally, dessert is served: an ultra-sweet dish made by Gabriel, consisting of fresh pineapple boiled in sugar, which we neutralize by drinking bitter Cuban coffee.

After dinner, there's only one way to get back to my *hostal*: walking. I thank Isabel and Marilys for their culinary efforts and stagger down the high front steps into the street. The houses in this neighborhood are all one-story and all attached to each other. They have no front yard, just a shuttered window with metal bars and a door fronting on the sidewalk. In Julian's case, there's no backyard either, since his son has used the backyard to build his own home by adding two rooms onto his father's house: a kitchen and a bedroom, one on top of the other.

As the sidewalks are unreliable, Julian, his son and I walk down the middle of the dimly lit streets in this residential area. The traffic is sparse and the air is cool, but still comfortable for short sleeves. Other people are walking in the street too, and faint music is coming from some of the doorways, which makes for a friendly, informal atmosphere.

"So what are your first impressions of Santa Clara?" asks Gabriel.

"Oh gosh, I haven't really seen it yet – it's been in the dark so far. It seems small and friendly – intimate," I answer, trying to be diplomatic.

"*Hostal Casita*, the place where you will sleep, is small and intimate too," adds Julian. "You know, I went to school with Teresita. We were in the same class together during our whole school time – she's my age precisely."

"Wow, that's really something. And you've kept in touch over the last, what, fifty years?"

"No, in fact we didn't. She studied physics, and she was a physics teacher in the secondary school before she retired. I just met her again when I was looking for a *hostal* for you. It's a small business: you are the only guest."

We walk around one end of the Parque Vidal, the *plaza mayor* of Santa Clara. There's suddenly music coming from a half dozen doorways, and I notice groups of people laughing and dancing in the street outside bars and restaurants.

"Maybe we could come here for a drink some evening. Would that be a good idea?" I ask. They acknowledge my suggestion with polite enthusiasm.

"We're almost at *Hostal Casita* now – it's just two blocks from Parque Vidal. You're lucky to be near the center," Gabriel says.

───── •••• ─────

It's nearly midnight by the time I have unpacked and am ready for bed. The temperature on this March evening has dropped considerably, so I dig out the two thin blankets from the bottom of the closet and throw them over my sheet and bedspread. It's going to be a chilly night with no glass in my window. How, I wonder, do most Cubans manage in low temperatures like these? They probably don't have many blankets. I get into the double bed, turn out the light and count my blessings: I've flown safely, survived a five-person official interrogation, been met at the airport, enjoyed a delicious meal among friends, and now I'm lying in a clean bed with enough blankets. Plus, I have my whole Cuba vacation before me.

On the other hand, I've had a glimpse of what can happen to people who say the wrong words and thus appear to be a threat to state power. In my case, the word was *iglesia* – church. I can't believe how fast it happened. One minute I was a happy camper, heading for sun and fun; the next, mistaken for a missionary, I was a suspect behind closed doors, being interrogated by five immigration officers. Would anyone have helped me if Julian hadn't been waiting? Would I have been held for further questioning? My fear of police tactics has increased, and my benevolence toward the regime has diminished. I've also had a glimpse of my own behavior under police questioning, and how the mere suggestion of a cross-examination made my mouth dry up and say whatever the young guards wanted to hear. Luckily they took the trouble to find Julian.

18
STRANGERS IN PARADISE

M Y FIRST NIGHT IN SANTA Clara is typical of all subsequent ones. First of all, it's bracingly cool, especially under the light bedding available. Second, since the windows are devoid of glass, my bedroom is full of outside noises. To be precise, night noises and morning noises. One bedroom window opens on the atrium or patio of my *hostal* and the other opens on the patio of the house next door, so I can hear faint snoring or else faint cries and comforting murmurs anytime I wake up. Towards morning, but before the sun has risen, I can also hear roosters crowing, buckets being filled at outdoor taps and horses trotting through the streets at some speed, presumably pulling carts. I'm not a light sleeper, so none of this bothers me; in fact, I love lying in bed, invisible and secure, surrounded by the sounds of a Cuban morning.

Ernesto's horn pierces the *hostal's* front door. It's 8 a.m. and by now I'm dressed, breakfasted and ready for our first excursion. Isabel is sitting in the front passenger seat so that Julian and I can speak English together in the back. Now I can observe Ernesto at work in daylight. He calmly cuts through rush-hour traffic as we work our way out of the city in his white Peugeot. The car's upholstery is a little the worse for wear, but Julian says there's air conditioning if required. Ernesto is mild-mannered and friendly as he chats with Isabel, who does most of the talking. He's about fifty, with short brown hair and glasses.

One problem I need to solve urgently is money – I don't have any CUCs. I ask to stop at a bank on our way out of Santa Clara, but Ernesto says it's easier to stop on our drive to the coast. He recommends the bank in Camajuani, about halfway to Remedios.

We pull up to the curb on Camajuani's main street. I note five parked horse carts and a small selection of unrefinished vintage cars. Will this place have a bank that can change four hundred Canadian dollars? I can see it's a real town with its own civic and commercial life: people have come here to do their shopping. But it's also a rural town, and people have time on their hands – time to lean into a car window and chat with the driver, for example. One such leaner is wearing knee-high rubber boots, muddy jeans and an old T-shirt, the back of which reads *Mas unidos, fuertes y solidarios que nunca* (More united, strong and supportive than ever). It looks as if he wore it to a demonstration three years ago and never took it off.

At the diminutive bank, a machine-gun-toting guard with a bulletproof vest opens the door and waves us in. Three local women are standing together at the teller's window, chatting away. When they see us, they step aside, motioning that we should take their place. Is this a rare event for them? Or are they just so polite that they let all foreigners go first? The teller changes my Canadian dollars to several hundred CUCs without batting an eye. Julian and I re-count the money together and then leave, bidding everybody "*Adios y gracias*". They all wave and say "*Adios*", including the armed guard at the door.

Our first excursion of the week is to the historic town of Remedios, which is forty kilometers – or about one hour – to the north of Santa Clara. When we get there, Ernesto parks in the shade on one side of the central square and says he'll be waiting for us there at noon. He seems about to clean his car, maybe do some light repairs, possibly some shopping. I notice that his lunch and water are packed in a cooler in the trunk. I also notice that he's wearing cropped pants and flip-flops; he's the most informally dressed of any of us.

Julian, Isabel and I are now on our own. Julian has been here many times as an interpreter with American and European church groups. He wants to show me the famous church and have a general look around. Isabel is from a nearby village and knows the town well. She's just come along for the ride – and also to see the coastal causeway in the afternoon. She's dressed up and wearing make up; I'm wearing Capri pants and sandals but no make up, and have a bathing suit and towel stowed in the bottom of my daypack.

Remedios is old and, like Trinidad, dates to around 1515. In other words, it was founded not too long after Columbus made landfall on Cuba, and a century before the Pilgrims hit Plymouth Rock. Being fairly near the coast, the two settlements used to be regularly attacked by pirates. In fact, people from Remedios went inland to found Santa Clara when they finally got fed up with pirate attacks. Unlike Trinidad, Remedios is a fairly quiet place with only one major monument: the rather humble-looking yellow stucco church of San Juan Bautista, alias St. John the Baptist. Julian, Isabel and I make a beeline for it.

Apart from its wall-to-wall glittering gold altar, and an ancient stone in the floor engraved with the names of the founding families, the church interior is rather plain. We've finished looking around it in about twenty minutes. A group of Californians on a peace mission are shuffling around the pews just like we are, so Julian and I fall into conversation with some of them. They've flown to Cuba via Mexico because of the ban on US citizens travelling to Cuba.

"So, which places in Cuba will you visit?" inquires Julian.

"Oh, a lot of places," answers one of them, a stocky lady with huge dangly earrings and one long braid of gray hair. "We started in Santiago – held a service of witness for the Guantanamo prisoners there – and then we flew here. A Cubana Airlines flight – heh heh, kinda different," she remarks to me, smiling meaningfully. "And now we're doing this bus tour gig, going to Havana, seeing some places in between. We usually have our evening meal with local folks wherever we stop."

"And are you satisfied with your visit?" Julian again, sounding like an interviewer from the ministry of tourism.

"Well, sometimes it's kinda hard to talk to people, you know? It's like there's this invisible barrier and it's hard to communicate across it? We have our facts, they have their facts, and even though we both want understanding, we're just, like, not on the same page? But I do believe – I really do – that the Cubans and us, we're coming closer."

We wish her well and sincerely hope she's right.

"OK, what else is Remedios famous for?" I ask as we cross the square next to the church.

"*Parrandas*," answers Julian and winks at Isabel, who assures me that *parrandas* are something *muy especial*. She explains that they're elaborate celebrations held at Christmas, involving two rival districts, which each construct a huge fireworks tower and a themed float. The festivities go on for days, culminating in a contest for the best float. Isabel becomes quite animated telling me about *las parrandas*, which are also a custom in her hometown of Zulueta. It sounds like a colorful custom, but I guess you have to live here to really appreciate it.

We have a little more time before we meet Ernesto, so we ask two bicitaxi drivers if they can take us on a tour of Remedios for half an hour or so. Since there's no way all three of us can fit into one bicitaxi, we hire them both for our tour. Isabel and I make up one passenger load and Julian the other. Our two drivers ride side by side so that we can all chat as we drive. There's no traffic to disturb our ride down the quiet streets.

The first two things I notice as we roll along unhurriedly are not tourist sights. One is that our driver is holding the handlebars with one hand and one wrist-stump. The other is that the streets beyond Remedios' central square are not paved. This town of several thousand inhabitants is based on dirt roads. The first stop on our slow and gentle tour is a rather run-down canning factory. Our drivers encourage us to descend and look through the large glassless windows, where something is being steamed and stewed and canned. The smell gives it away: '*Tomates,*' says Isabel. The drivers beam broad smiles, as if they've shown us something we've always wanted to see.

"Yes it's the tomato season now," says our driver to Isabel. "They do tomatoes for two, three weeks and then fruits start: *guayaba*, plums, peaches, and so on."

"*Si si*, in Santa Clara too," answers Isabel knowledge-ably. She is very good at small talk.

"I used to work in that factory," says our driver. "It's a good place to work – not too hard. But then I had my accident." And he waves his wrist in the air to show us what he's talking about.

"Sssss!" Isabel draws her breath between her teeth, but is not afraid to ask the inevitable question. "*Que paso?*"

"*Las Parrandas...,*" he shrugs ruefully, "a big firecracker went off in my hand."

"*Jesus-Maria!*" exclaims Isabel. "*Si, si, parrandas* are dangerous. I know – I'm from Zulueta myself."

After further patrolling the quiet side-streets and even getting a sneak preview of next December's *parranda* float, we finally trundle back to the main square, passing the only department store in town, poetically called *La Ilusion*. What a wonderful name, I say to myself, instantly struck by its surrealistic truth. The whole town feels like an illusion, a mirage lost in time, well insulated from the world's getting and spending.

But the illusion is soon to be shattered. As noon strikes, a dozen cars, twice as many bikes and a hundred uniformed school children all appear out of nowhere and tear around or across the central square on their way home to lunch. It's time for our rendez-vous with Ernesto. We point out the white Peugeot waiting across the square and are dropped off beside the car.

———————•••———————

Ernesto first takes us through Caibarien, an old seaside town with character, which I hope someday to visit properly. After that we are stopped at a check-point barrier, where the guards check my passport and the others' IDs and we pay a small fee. The barrier lifts and we start out for the keys – or *cayeria* as Isabel calls it – the chain of tiny islands that extends fifty kilometers into the Atlantic. The view is breathtaking: absolutely flat turquoise water as far as the eye can see and we are driving out into the middle of it. The narrow causeway, which includes a series of bridges, makes us feel as if we are sailing out from islet to islet. White beaches or mangrove stands line the shore. There's no traffic; in fact, no sound except the cries of gulls and herons.

Ernesto, the only one of us who's been here before, first takes us to Cayo Las Brujas, which offers beach access for day tourists and has a restaurant with a wonderful view of the sea. Once again, he drops us off and disappears discreetly, saying he'll be back in two hours. We're hungry by this time, and the restaurant has windows on three sides, so we enter to have lunch with a view. Business is slow: only two other tables are occupied. The menu offers little choice, but we take the daily special for a surprisingly reasonable price. "Ice cream, diverse flavors" is listed as the dessert. When we ask what diverse flavors there are, we are told "Strawberry". It's so typical that I have to swallow a chuckle.

And now for the beach. Still a gorgeous turquoise, the water beckons as I kick off my sandals and dig my toes into the sand. There's no one else on this palm-lined, white beach, which is several kilometers long. Where is everybody? I wonder if I should change into my bathing suit here or go back to the toilet in the restaurant. Julian and Isabel clearly have no intention of getting wet; they've kept their shoes on and look distinctly uncomfortable. Just then, I spy two plastic sunbeds and drag them into the shade of a palm tree, side-by-side. My two strangers in their own land follow me and obediently take their assigned seats, fully clothed, looking out to sea. The beach is not what they came for, but they'll put up with it to humor me.

I can't wait to get my feet in the water. As I wade in up to my knees, I notice how very shallow it is. I won't be able to swim even if I do put on my bathing suit. The water's lovely and warm though. Since we've still got an hour here, I decide to leave my daypack with Julian and Isabel, walk as far as I can in half an hour, and then turn back. I walk at the waterline, where the sand is firmest and the water cools my feet. At first there's not a soul on the beach. Then I notice a distant figure, possibly in uniform, coming towards me. It is a uniform – and a gun: a policeman patrolling the beach. For criminals? For tourists?

"*Buenos dias*," I say as we pass each other.

"*Buenos dias*," he replies from behind his silver sunglasses, not stopping.

I continue to pick up the odd shell and slip it into my pocket, conscious now of possibly being observed. The sea and sky are only slightly different in color, and, with the water so smooth, it's sometimes hard to make out where they meet. I'm standing alone, horizon-less, up to my knees in paradise, with a strange sense of alienation. Where are all the people?

On my way back, I come across four young women, setting up for a picnic on the beach. They're speaking English, so I stop for a chat.

"Nice place for a picnic," I start.

"Yeah, we'd thought we'd get away on our own for a change." They're from England.

"Why? You staying at a hotel out here?"

"Yes, out at the far end – you know, at Cayo Santa Maria there?"

"Yeah – I mean I've never been out there, but I've seen it on a map – it must be spectacular."

"Yeah, well, it is fantastic, but everything's so organized, you know? Buffet meals, pool, entertainment... We thought we'd like to stay in touch with the real world, so we took a taxi here to have a good old picnic on the beach for a change." They all giggle. I know what they mean. Resort vacations can be so well organized that they're no fun anymore.

"But why *this* beach?" I want to know.

"Well, this is the only beach where it's allowed – at least that's what our taxi guy said."

"You mean the beaches are kept free of tourists?"

"Well, obviously not in the resorts, but outside the resorts, yes. It seems there're only a few places where you can just plunk your gear down and go swimming or have a picnic."

I can just about pick out Isabel and Julian waiting on their shady sunbeds, so I continue my homeward wade, mulling over this strange tourist-free stretch of paradise between foreigner-filled Cayo Santa Maria and Cuban Camajuani.

Ernesto's final stop on the long *cayeria* causeway is Cayo Ensenachos, where he thinks we'll like the mini-mall for tourists as much as he does. Actually it's not much of a shopping mall – just a double row of market stalls with local handicrafts, plus a few souvenir shops, restaurants and cafés. Isabel and I head for the toilets, which are for once up to North American standards. Compared to the toilets in the Las Brujas restaurant, they are paragons of cleanliness. I show Isabel how to get water from the sensor tap, and somehow want to take credit for the soap and paper towels, too. "You see? This is what a toilet should be like," I want to say, "Clean and well equipped." I hope she's impressed.

Julian is waiting across the street in front of a café. "Should we have a coffee?" he suggests. He's taking care of his women. The café is decorated to suggest a Parisian nightclub like the Moulin Rouge. We seat ourselves at a ridiculously small table and order. The coffee arrives almost at once, obviously made before we entered. Isabel tastes it and wrinkles her nose.

"It's terrible," she whispers, "much too weak." Julian and I drink the percolated dishwater without a murmur, but Isabel can't get over it.

"How can they serve that? It's not real Cuban coffee," she says. And she keeps repeating this verdict for the rest of the day.

Probably if you were to ask Isabel – even today – what she remembers about her visit to the tourist mall at Ensenachos, she'd say the coffee was bad. If you asked me, on the other hand, I'd say the toilets were among the best I've experienced in Cuba. And that's interesting. It seems to have something to do with our expectations. I expect clean toilets as a minimum standard, and if they're not clean, I'm disappointed – indignant even. In the same way, Isabel expects good coffee as her minimum standard, so she's angry if it's weak, whereas my expectations for coffee are not quite so high. I like good coffee, but I don't get mad if it's a little less than good. It's probably a cultural difference and therefore worth knowing about if you're in the tourist business.

Still with some time on our hands Isabel, Julian and I climb a three-story look-out tower at the far end of the mall. From the top we can see hundreds of swim-suited tourists walking on the beach or jumping into the ocean. Behind them, away from the water, are hotels and smaller residential units surrounded by gardens and a network of paths. I want to go and have a look, so I zoom back down the stairs and open a door in the wall that seems to lead to where I want to go. Two armed guards are waiting on the other side. They take one look at me and know I don't belong there. "Sorry," they say politely, and wave me back towards the door. It's then that I notice the identification bracelets on the other tourists' wrists. They belong there and I don't. I belong in no man's land. Or in the world at the end of the causeway.

So, instead of gaining admission to the tourist ghetto, we walk up and down the souvenir stalls: T-shirts and flip-flops, carved wooden hummingbirds and chess sets, leather belts and hats. I am put off by the crassness of some of the items, but Ernesto, who materializes out of thin air, buys a leather cowboy hat, bargaining down the price to ten CUCs. He's always wanted one, he says, and wears it for the rest of the week.

On the way home we stop to buy fruit at an unmarked house known to Ernesto as a place of high quality at low prices. Isabel goes in with him, while Julian and I stay in the car.

"Ernesto certainly knows where to buy things," I comment.

"Yes, he does," agrees Julian. "He's always looking for ehm a good deal."

"And that was a really gorgeous beach where we had lunch today," I continued. "It was strange that there was no one there. In Europe, a sandy beach like that with warm, turquoise water would be crowded with people."

"Yes, well, you saw the crowds at Ensenachos."

"But I mean *we* weren't allowed on the beach at Ensenachos. It's as if they want to keep tourists apart from Cubans and maybe even apart from tourists like me. What do you think?"

"Heh heh. You are very observant. The ehm powers-that-be think tourists will corrupt us."

"Corrupt you! How would they do that?"

"With their money, with their materialism – giving tips and so on."

"But if the tourists just stay on those islands fifty kilometers from the Cuban coast, the government gets all their money. Nothing comes here to normal, everyday Cuba."

"Yes, that's right. The government gets the tourists' money and protects us from corruption." It's not really a laughing matter, but we both grin and shrug our shoulders. What else can we do?

When I get back to my room at *Hostal Casita* that evening, I switch on my mini-TV, up in its place above the fridge. The main item on the news is the death from cancer of Hugo Chavez, Venezuela's president. Cuba announces three days of national mourning. The newsreaders are all wearing black ties. People are shown crying in the streets. Why on earth are they crying for such an idiot, I wonder. I don't know much about him, but I've read about his imprudent policies in The Economist. I also remember seeing news footage of him speaking to the UN General Assembly, making a fool of himself on the podium by pretending, with religious gestures, to exorcise the devilish aura left behind by George W. Bush. I never cared for Bush as a president, but I couldn't respect Chavez' clowning either.

19
EXPLORING SANTA CLARA

J ULIAN'S FORMER SCHOOLMATE, TERESITA, IS already working noiselessly in the kitchen when I emerge from my bedroom to have breakfast on the *Casita* patio, the open-roofed area of the house that is lined with small palm trees, blooming orchids, and canaries singing in their cages. Smiling and dignified, Teresita glides in from the kitchen with a tray of tea, rolls and sliced tropical fruit. Her two grandsons, aged about 10 and 14, have already emerged from their bedroom and are sulkily eating breakfast in the kitchen before going to school; only Teresita's canaries break the silence, warbling to each other across the patio.

After the boys have gone off, Teresita comes back from the kitchen to see if I want anything else. I don't, so she sits down to socialize a bit, quizzing me on our plans for the day. What time is Julian coming? Where are we going? Her Spanish is slow and very clear; mine is just slow. She can even say a few words in English, although she prefers not to. We regard each other across the table:

two gray-haired women, both modern and educated, both teachers, both active and competent, both supposedly retired but juggling more responsibilities than ever; we understand each other immediately and feel mutual respect. I find out that Teresita is José's mother-in-law. Her daughter works at a government-owned all-night gas station. It's a desirable job because she earns a salary in CUCs; the downside is that she frequently has to work twenty-four-hour shifts. Teresita has therefore taken over her daughter's home duties: helping the boys get ready for school, getting most of the meals, taking care of the *hostal* laundry and cleaning, talking to guests. She also gives private lessons in physics in the afternoons.

Hostal Casita is conveniently located near the center of this city of well over 200,000 souls. The train station is not far either, and I hear the lonesome hooting of night trains when I lie in bed. In the one-way street directly outside our front door, cars and bicycles drive by regularly, although not often enough to prevent children from playing soccer in the street after school. Nearby, narrow horse-drawn trams called *carretone*s ply their routes, transporting up to eight passengers at a time. There are also buses, regular taxis, scooter-taxis and *bicitaxis*, but they are few and far between. Although Santa Clara is big as Cuban cities go, it feels more like a town than a city. People usually walk to where they want to go. Sidewalks are narrow or non-existent, so most people walk in the street whenever they can.

Today Julian has planned a walking tour of his hometown. He and his son Gabriel pick me up. They chat with José for ten minutes, even though they aren't close friends. Cubans have social skills the Swiss can only dream of. We step out into the street under a steel-blue winter sky. The night was unusually cool – under ten degrees centigrade – but the sun will soon have us sweating.

"We propose to do two things this morning," says Gabriel, who's clearly proud of his organizing. "First, we'll walk out to the Loma del Capiro, a hill on the outskirts of Santa Clara and then back into town, to visit the market. In reality it's two markets across the street from each other. They're very different – and maybe it'll be interesting for you from an economic or touristic viewpoint."

"OK. Sounds good." I try to keep things light.

"Well, Heather, did you sleep well last night?" asks Julian. "It was very cold."

"I slept fine. Really well." I answer. "I like cool temperatures for sleeping. I found two blankets in the closet of my room."

"Well, I had to wear my pajamas, a shirt, a sweater, a jacket and a scarf to bed." I make a mental note to bring a fleece blanket on my next visit to Cuba.

After following a busy road for about fifteen minutes, we come upon a slightly larger-than-life bronze statue of Che, in uniform and boots, holding a small child on his arm and a cigar in the other hand. Taking advantage of the photo op, we pose for and take pictures of each other.

"The statue is called *Che de los Ninos* because of the children. See them on his shoulder and his belt? It's a symbolic statue," explains Julian.

"What's this big building behind us?" I ask.

"The Santa Clara Communist Party – it's their headquarters."

"Oh. It sure is quiet. Not too much going on today, I guess." Neither man comments. I don't try to make another joke.

A couple of broiling kilometers more and we are approaching the grassy hill that is our goal, the Loma del Capiro. It's only 150 meters high, but we're huffing and puffing by the time we reach the top. On the way up we pass a team of female gardeners, middle-aged and over, who greet us as we walk by. They're planting shrubs and replacing some of the concrete steps. One of them has a grandchild with her; she's child-minding while she works. The huge flags on the top of the Loma are flying at half-mast.

"Ah yes. The flags are for Hugo Chavez. He died yesterday," says Gabriel.

"Mhm. That is certainly the reason," agrees his father.

"It's surprising that Cuba should do that for the president of another country," I comment.

"Chavez was a good friend," says Gabriel. "He ended the "special period in a time of peace" by sending us oil and money. Venezuela and Cuba became very close after that. All Cubans are in mourning."

"Heather, listen, I want to tell you something historical," interrupts Julian, "this is where the battle of Santa Clara started. I remember it well – I was sixteen at the time. Che and his men were approaching from Caibarien in the north, and the train from Havana with Batista's troops and ammunition had come the way we walked today. But Batista's men were tired of fighting. Still, the only way the rebels could stop the train and capture the ammunition was to use surprise tactics..."

And then I hear the story of Che's famous attack on the armored train again. I can picture it, and it was brilliant, but somehow it's not as stirring for me as it seems to be for them. I listen politely but keep my eyes lifted to the insanely bright blue sky behind the flags.

The concrete hulk of the state-run agricultural market looks deserted but isn't. Inside, customers wait in a slow-moving line for subsidized potatoes. It's dark in here and quiet. The would-be customers shuffle along grimly. People are just there to get the potatoes allotted to them by their *libreta*. They come with their own bags or else have bought a plastic bag outside for a few centavos. There's nothing else for sale: no beans, no onions – only disgracefully mud-covered potatoes.

Across the road, the colorful private market could not be more of a contrast. It first attracts, then overwhelms us with the loud shouting of its vendors and the sheer variety of produce: carrots, beans, sweet potatoes, yucca, onions, garlic, peppers… We sample pineapple slices, and I discover the super-sweet, pink-fleshed *mamey*. We buy one for dessert sometime. And, of course, several *guayabas* for me, their fragrance still irresistible.

To return to town, we board a nearly full eight-passenger *carreton*, first handing up our bags of shopping to other passengers and then, when properly seated at the back, passing our peso fare forward to the driver. With us his vehicle is full, so he flicks his whip over the horse's ears and we're off towards the center of town again. We've taken a *carreton* that serves the route to the hospitals.

Passengers tell the driver exactly where they want to get off along the way. During our ride under shady canvas, I notice ground floor windowsills with canned and bottled drinks lined up on them. Gabriel explains that house-owners have recently been granted permission to sell soft drinks from their front windows. Another small step towards a market-driven economy.

———————— ••• ————————

Julian wants to have lunch at *NaturArte*, a new restaurant and park-like enterprise he's heard of. It seems to me that the owner must have received some kind of government subsidy, because I've never seen a Cuban private business on this scale. It employs at least twenty young men and women, and they're working hard taking care of birds and fish, watering trees and plants, cleaning up a glass dump once used by the hospital, running the restaurant, and selling garden ornaments and cement. It's scaled like a European or American garden center, yet appears to have almost no customers.

The owner introduces himself and shows us some examples of the art in *NaturArte*: a life-size bronze statue of Che Guevara and a huge bronze blue heron. Who, I wonder, is going to buy them? Will people want a Che statue in their garden? It doesn't appear to matter. Either the man has another source of income or he plans to make all his profit on bus tours stopping for lunch. The spacious outdoor restaurant is bounded on its four sides by the bar, a kitchen counter, a wrought-iron gate and a bamboo forest. As it's new, we're not surprised that we're the only guests. Best of all, even with prices in CUCs, the food is reasonable and delicious.

Our conversation is mostly about Cuba's current situation. It's exciting for father and son to observe how fast things are changing economically. Who would have thought, even three years ago, that such a restaurant and leisure park would exist and be owned by one man? He's obviously working within the law, but I keep thinking he must have some kind of powerful backing. Let's hope there are enough people who want to come here and be amused. My two companions guess that some people in Santa Clara might be rich enough to come here for dinner "once or twice a year".

Later in the afternoon, Julian, Gabriel and I take over a bench in the Parque Vidal, the green heart of Santa Clara. As parks go, it's perhaps not the lushest, but it's certainly among the busiest outside Havana. A bronze statue of Marta Abreu, the great 19th century benefactress of Santa Clara, sits in a chair at one end, observing the antics of her benefactees. Across the street from the park, workmen are slowly constructing a stage and installing a sound system in front of the Palacio Provincial Marti, which is the home of the municipal library. The building is the grandest of all the neo-classic constructions lining the Parque, with its creamy-white two-story columns and balconied windows. The Provincial Palace will house the Santa Clara book of condolences for Chavez' death, to be sent to Venezuela with dozens of others from all over Cuba. The book will lie open for signing by ordinary citizens for two days and two nights, Julian tells me.

We discuss what Chavez' death means for Cuba's

future. I can hear that my friends are worried. There are many thousands of Cubans in Venezuela, working as doctors, nurses, teachers, sports coaches, technicians. What if they all have to come home? Cuba is desperately dependent on Venezuela for oil, without which it will come grinding to a halt as it did in the early 1990s, when the Soviet Union disintegrated. The "special period" traumatized Cubans, and the present threat of a recurrence is awakening traumatic memories.

We continue to sit and people-watch, drinking bottled water and discussing God and the world. Gabriel and I are atheists – well, maybe agnostics; Julian is a Christian, but not as involved in church matters as when Nelson was alive. We all want world peace; we want Guantanamo to be returned to Cuba; we want the US embargo to end.

No one around us seems to be in a hurry. Passersby stop and help the workmen in front of the Palacio Provincial by handing up boards and equipment. Young people stroll past in semi-embrace, wearing purpose-ripped jeans and tight Lycra tops. Toddlers chase pigeons while mothers chat. Schoolchildren in their maroon and white uniforms, holding a parent or grandparent by the hand, make their way home from school.

Two thin men in their eighties approach and, one after the other, ask me for pens or soap. They think the three of us are tourists and that I, as a woman, will be the most compassionate. An elderly woman, all hair and wrinkles, takes a seat on the bench opposite, the better to observe me as I sit chatting with my friends. I assume she will eventually ask me for money, too, but I am wrong. When we leave I realize she's been waiting for me to finish my bottle of water. She retrieves it from the garbage basket for the ten-cent deposit.

———————————

Later in the week, I get to experience Santa Clara by night with Gabriel and his wife, Marilys. They pick me up in the early evening and we walk the two blocks back to Parque Vidal, which, as they predicted, is full of young people and the young at heart. Music streams from bars and cafés across the street from the park and there's a professional-sounding brass band practicing in the bandstand. Outside a darkened cinema, three rock musicians are playing their amplified version of Rock Around The Clock, and couples in their forties and fifties are dancing in the street before about twenty onlookers. I invite my companions for a drink. For some reason they choose a soulless café with Formica surfaces next door to the Santa Clara Libre hotel. We drink beer and I ask questions about what they usually do in the evening. From their answers I gather that going out more than once a week, even for a one-dollar beer, is too expensive for them. The café closes at nine, and we're in the street once more. We poke our heads into other places, where dancers are doing something more graceful than the lindy. Everyone's having fun on as little money as possible.

The next morning, I wake up early and walk back to the Parque Vidal with my camera to take pictures in the early morning light. On my way, I pass a shoemaker, working outdoors in the small space in front of his house – his outdoor workshop. His greeting is drowned out by a woman advertising her wares. She shouts, "*Veneno para cucarachas, ratones, hormigas*" ("Poison for cockroaches, rats, ants"), which she appears to be carrying in a cloth bag on her shoulder.

When I get to the park, there's a surprising amount of activity. *Bicitaxis* are more in evidence. The most stylish of them now offer the added value of colored lights and music from a ghetto-blaster behind the seat. Women in spandex shorts and sandals with six-inch heels are dropped off from the back of motor scooters and go into the Post Office. Men wear work-worn jeans and T-shirts, as if dressed to spend the day laboring. Compared with men in Havana, they seem less aware of their appearance. Flower sellers, their delicate wares placed in giant cans of water, line up on the far side of the park. People are not too poor to spend a few pesos on a small bouquet.

Pictures taken, I turn back towards my *hostal*. In a side street I notice an older lady strolling along, taking the air with a parrot on her shoulder. It's attached to a fine chain she's holding, so it can't fly away. The lady and the parrot are scouting the neighborhood together, turning their heads in synch to follow the movements of passersby – and even those of nondescript dogs reconnoitering the gutters. Julian has told me that his wife feeds most of the derelict dogs in their neighborhood, giving them names when necessary. There are quite a few deserving candidates near my *hostal*, too.

One street-corner has been converted into a walled park the size of a small house. It's a solid concrete park, more appropriate for skipping rope or bouncing balls off walls. And the walls are what make the park special: a local artist has painted a mural with silhouettes of the four Beatles on them. I'm struck by nostalgia to see young John, Paul, George and Ringo marching along, straight out of the sixties. But what does the mural say to Cubans? Is it an allusion to international pop culture, or is it a reminder of the early years after the revolution?

20
FROM TOCOROROS TO TRINIDAD

O N OUR NEXT OUTING WITH Ernesto, this time
to the mountains, we soon run into trouble:
there's been an accident up ahead on a narrow
bridge. A dozen cars and trucks are lined up in front of us
on this dusty country road, waiting to cross. It looks like
a side-collision between a yellow school bus and a truck.

The atmosphere is tense. Some drivers get out of
their cars and walk to the bridge. Others just drum their
fingers on the car roof, impatient to be moving again.
Unusually for Cuba, there's no music pulsing from any
of the vehicles; this is because Cuba is in the midst of a
three-day mourning period for Venezuela's Hugo Chavez
and all public music has stopped. Suddenly, all the drivers
in front of us start their motors and roar off to the left,
over a bumpy field, towards a secondary road. Some cars
behind us do this, too. Ernesto sits tight, his round face
impassive, his eyes on the bridge. When the dust of the
departing vehicles has cleared, he calmly starts the motor
and slowly rolls up to the bridge just as the truck backs

HEATHER MURRAY

off, leaving the bus – its side torn away – waiting to be towed. We squeeze past the bus, the first car to cross the bridge. Nobody's been hurt, and it isn't a real school bus anyway, but a donated Canadian bus that was being used for passenger transport. I let out my breath, which I've been holding for fear of seeing injured children.

Today's excursion is to take us into the highest mountains in the province, the Sierra de Escambray, where we'll walk in a forested national park, and then visit the picturesque town of Trinidad on the south coast before returning to home base in Santa Clara. It's the excursion I've been looking forward to most since Julian first wrote to me proposing daytrips with a chauffeur. That's because my guidebook says that there are a number of hiking trails in the park.

There are just three of us in the car: Julian, Ernesto and myself. Ernesto speaks not a word of English, so he and I are reduced to communicating either in elementary Spanish or via Julian. Sometimes Ernesto makes a stab at conversation:

"*Edder,* (Ernesto's name for me) *hay cabras en Suiza?*"

"*Cabras?* Julian, *Julian* – what does *cabras* mean?" Julian is absorbed in my Cuban guidebook and needs surfacing time to deal with my question.

"*Cabras?* Well, ehm, they could be goats,... or possibly...."

"Oh goats! *Si, si, Ernesto, hay cabras en Suiza. Como no? Pero, no hay tantas cabras como vacas.*" I give him the scintillating information that there are indeed goats in Switzerland, but not nearly as many goats as cows. This is

252

the sort of foreign language conversation I normally try to avoid, but I'll talk about anything to get closer to Ernesto.

We drive through a string of rural villages and then turn off onto a narrow, winding, potholed and traffic-free road to the top of a pass in the Escambray. Cool spring water gushes from moss on both sides. "*Agua de paradiso*" Ernesto calls it and stops the car just to enjoy the sound and the cool air. Birds coo and twitter. My ears pop: we are about 800 meters above sea level.

"This is heaven for me," he tells us, breathing deeply with all the car windows down. "When it's really muggy in the summer, we pack a lunch and I bring my family up here. We just sit in the shade, have a picnic... and wait till it's cooler in Santa Clara."

Just then a huge open-backed truck approaches from the opposite direction. As it rattles past, taking up most of the road, we notice that its back is crammed with twenty or more terrified-looking tourists in sunhats, standing and holding on for dear life. Both Julian and Ernesto chuckle.

"They are having the complete Cuban experience," grins Julian. Ernesto tells us that the tourists are being taken to the top of a waterfall and will walk back to the nature center in an hour and a half. I'd like to do a walk like that, too, but don't think my two companions have planned anything that long.

A short drive later we are in Topes de Collantes, a quiet mountain resort first developed by Batista as the location of a large TB sanatorium, and later by the Castro brothers as an education center. The sanatorium – now a hotel – is still the main building today, sixty years later.

It was obviously renovated for East German tourists at some time after the revolution, because it still bears the name *Kurhaus*, which is German for spa hotel, chiseled in stone over the door.

"Can you imagine," says Julian, who is now in lecture-mode, "in the early time of the revolution, Fidel decided to relocate the national teacher-training center to this place, so trainees would be isolated from external influences and could concentrate better. Unfortunately, as in... heh heh... as in many other cases, reality did not live up to *El Maximo Lider's* expectations. There were sex scandals, and the usual transport problems... and the whole project became too expensive and impractical, and finally it was definitively abandoned." Cuba appears to be a land of abandoned projects.

Ernesto parks the car on a shady shoulder so we can visit the Casa de Café, where we're revived by aromatic cups of locally grown, freshly roasted coffee. A man of many connections, Ernesto has recognized a second cousin serving coffee there, who comes to sit with us at our table. Our coffees are on the house.

Topes de Collantes really is like paradise – not too hot, yet full of tropical trees and plants, birds and butterflies. It's a pity that Cuban mountain tourism is so underdeveloped. I'm not a serious bird-watcher, but I had tried, unsuccessfully, to order books on Cuban birds and national parks before this trip to Cuba. The only book available was decades old and not in color. How great it would be if the Casa de Café sold books on Cuba's geology, flora and fauna. But it doesn't, so tourists find little to do in this "nature center" except have a coffee and use the toilet. Then they go off in a truck for a carefully monitored woodland hike with a guide. As we drink our coffee, a steady stream of Tilley-hatted and hiking-sandaled Canadian eco-tourists, followed by similarly clad Italians and Germans, all head for the single toilet at the back of the Casa, which has probably been out of toilet paper since last week.

Ernesto announces that now we're going on a hike too, so the three of us set off along the road down to a river, leaving the other tourists in the Casa de Café. Then we cross the river on stepping-stones and enter the tropical forest on a narrow, bamboo-strewn path that Ernesto seems to know well. We follow the path up the hillside for about twenty minutes, Ernesto in the lead, me two steps behind, and Julian bringing up the rear at some distance. Ernesto doesn't say much, but when he sees that I'm interested, often stops to point out a flower or a particular tree or fruit. Suddenly, I hear strange, chuckling birdsong somewhere ahead of us. Ernesto grabs my arm, whispering excitedly and pointing.

"*Edder. Tocororo! Tocororo!*" My brain goes on red alert. Have I heard him right? The *tocororo* is the national bird of Cuba, exotic in color and form. Ernesto is pointing at a branch about twenty feet away. I ease my camera out of my daypack, keeping my eyes on the branch indicated. And then I spot it: a medium-sized bird with a white breast, cherry-red belly, indigo back and long, gracefully forked tail.

"*Lo ves bien?*" whispers Ernesto.

"*Si, si,*" I can see it well, I reply, clicking away. I've taken a half dozen shots and am squinting at the back of my digital camera when Julian comes stomping up the path behind us.

"Ernesto," he calls in Spanish, "you saw a bird? A *tocororo*? That is indeed something special – where is it?" and crashes past us, walking right under the bird, which naturally flies away. Ernesto and I exchange resigned glances in silence.

It is situations like these that reveal the fault-lines of friendship. Up to today, I had assumed that Julian shared my love of the wild, that he, as an educated, well-read person, would also know some names of common plants and animals, that he would know how to observe wildlife and how to walk through the forest without causing noise or damage. But I was mistaken: he is not interested in trees or birds the way I am. Inconceivably for me, he doesn't know the name of even one plant we've seen today. At this moment in the forest I feel that I have more in common with Ernesto than with Julian, even though Ernesto and I can barely communicate. Of course, Julian is still my great and good friend, with whom I share many other interests and values, but I have discovered an area – a big one for me – where our tastes, sadly, do not overlap.

On our return from the *tocororo* mini-safari, the three of us encounter an elderly man sitting on a bench near where we left the car. He greets us politely, and Julian and Ernesto start chatting with him right away. The man is wearing a black military beret with small medals pinned to it. Julian leans close to me and mutters, "He's a veteran of the revolution." Ernesto has just asked him where he fought, so I tune in to hear him answer that he was in a brigade that fought in the battle of Santa Clara.

Veterans have the right to stay at the big hotel in Topes de Collantes for next to nothing. When he hears Julian explaining this to me in English, the veteran asks me if I'm from Canada. When I say "Yes, from Nova Scotia," he tells me he once worked on a ship that made regular trips to Montreal and back. He knows Halifax well. Julian and Ernesto raise their eyebrows, smile and nod their heads as we get into the car; they seem as impressed with meeting an authentic hero of the revolution as I am with spotting a *tocororo*.

***

Our walk in the Escambray forest lasted little more than an hour, but Ernesto says it's time to start our descent to Trinidad on the south coast. The drive provides thrills in the form of a twenty percent gradient and sharp curves that force even an experienced driver like Ernesto to brake to ten miles per hour. This slow pace is altogether welcome, however, because it affords long views of the mountains melting into the coastal plain, of emerald rectangles of sugar cane and, ultimately, of the pearly, light blue Caribbean twinkling through the haze below.

In about ninety minutes we're entering the town of Trinidad, with its cobbled streets and well-preserved colonial center. Here Julian comes to life again. He appreciated the mountain air of the Escambray, but history – especially Cuban history – is his forte.

"Well, Heather," he begins as we enter town, "what you see here are restored mansions from the eighteenth and nineteenth centuries. Yes, that was when Trinidad was most prosperous from sugar and tobacco, and when the plantation system ehm... flourished – with many slaves. The landowners were mostly from Spain, but some were French colonists from Haiti – you know, after the slaves revolted there. The French also built a number of mansions in and around Trinidad."

Ernesto has to park about two hundred meters below the Plaza Mayor. By now the sun is glaring down. We trudge uphill on the shady side of the street, taking in the recently restored colonial mansions, many of them now converted into bed-and-breakfasts or antique and souvenir shops. On this day of national mourning, however, Trinidad's narrow cobblestone lanes are silent, deliberately doing without the music that is usually played to attract tourists. I step over a scrawny black dog lying in the shade and catch up with Ernesto at the corner. He's watching two youths who are playing chess in silence, just sitting there on the sidewalk making move after move.

Finally, we arrive at La Botija, a restaurant that has been recommended to Ernesto by a fellow taxi driver. The name refers to the clay water-jug that slaves drank from when they worked in the fields on sugar plantations. And, as I gradually realize to my horror, slavery is the restaurant's theme, with waiters dressed in torn pajama-like garments and white headbands. The walls are decorated with whips and manacles, slave-purchase contracts and leg irons. The pièce de résistance is a long chain running the length of the dining room, fitted with eight neck irons used in the transport of slaves. Did they walk off the ship in a line, chained together at the neck? I picture it for the first time in my life. As Ernesto helpfully points out each of these attractions for my benefit, I feel worse and worse, but try not to show it. It's all I can do to order my meal. The waiters in their ragged slave outfits – all jaunty young men – seem oblivious to the horror that surrounds them.

Trying to muster some appetite and keep my eyes away from the accusing walls, I look at Ernesto and notice that he's weeping quietly behind his glasses while watching the small television perched above our table. He says he's sorry, but the death of Chavez makes him so sad that he can hardly eat. The TV is showing hundreds of Venezuelans silently paying their respects to Hugo Chavez, as they file past his open coffin in Caracas. Julian says he feels like crying, too, because Chavez was such a kind man – a man like Princess Diana. And so the three of us sit there, eating a wordless late lunch in a slave-themed restaurant in Trinidad. They are mourning the loss of a national hero, while I am weighed down by the cruelty of slavery. For the rest of the meal we are friends joined together in mute sadness.

———————

On our drive home, we stop off at the historic sugar plantation Manaca-Iznaga in la Valle de los Ingenios – the valley of the sugar mills. Thanks to La Botija, I can now clearly picture how the slaves were brought here, fastened together neck and foot, and how they were bought and sold and driven and prodded like cattle, all in order to earn fortunes for the Spanish and French mansion owners in Trinidad.

Julian and I climb the plantation's rocket-shaped tower, where I remember chasing after the Korean students four years earlier. From the top we watch the valley's steam train pull into the tiny station and pick up tourists. Then I turn to the north and make out the hazy Escambray mountains, where we saw the *tocororo*. I'd so much rather be there.

"Well, did you enjoy the walk today at Topes?" Julian inquires, as if reading my mind.

"Yes, I loved it," I say. "I can't believe I saw a *tocororo* on my very first walk in the jungle."

"Then I am happy," he says, "We will go again."

Back at the *hostal,* I show José and Teresita my trophy picture of the *tocororo*, which has to be zoomed quite a lot before they can see anything. We talk about the beauties of Trinidad – the pastel colors of the mansions, the ornate *plaza mayor*, the fine furniture, the cobbled streets.

"I was there twelve years ago," recalls Teresita. I realize once again how very lucky I am to have been there twice in four years.

"Do you like the mountains more than the seaside?" she asks.

Hmm, good question, I think. Then I say: "*Las montanas tienen mas vida que la playa, y...y me gusta observar las diferentes formas de vida.*" (The mountains have more life than the beach, and I like observing different forms of life.)

After supper, I step out the front door and turn right for an evening stroll. Making my way towards the Parque Vidal, I come upon clusters of policemen and barricades, then hundreds of people standing in the dimly lit streets all around the square. They have formed a huge queue, four or five people wide, and are waiting their turn to sign the Chavez condolence book. They converse in hushed voices as the line shuffles forward imperceptibly; some will have to wait until after midnight.

I wonder why Cubans put so much effort into expressing condolences that will never be received on a personal level. Do they regard it as an act of patriotism? Or is it an expression of their gratitude towards Chavez and his country for rescuing them from the "special period"? Or possibly just a matter of doing something with other Cubans on a historic occasion?

Back in my room, I switch on my television again. Cuban TV is showing nothing but Chavez re-runs. I sit down on my bed and start to watch. One newsreel shows Chavez in military uniform, holding a Cuban boy on his lap. He talks to the kid, listens to his answers, jokes with him, tousles his hair. I watch Chavez talking to athletes, Chavez signing an agreement with Fidel, Chavez joking with reporters. He wasn't such an idiot, actually – he could talk to anybody. And he really did empathize with his fellow humans. Julian was right: Chavez had a lot in common with Princess Diana.

21
LAKE HANABANILLA
AND FRIENDSHIP

BAROSO CUTS THE MOTOR, ALLOWING us to appreciate the silence, a stillness punctured only by the peeps and quacks of birds swimming in the coves. The lakeshore is steep in most places, either golden limestone, or jungle, or a grassy slope with random palms. My eye follows this steepness all the way up to the mountain peaks encircling the lake. Pico San Juan is the highest at over a thousand meters. With the motor silent, we can also hear the oars of a small boat some distance away. Two tourist fishermen out with rod and reel to catch the lake's abundant bass and trout.

Lake Hanabanilla is the size of a national park. Julian had mentioned going to a reservoir lake, but I hadn't expected this long, winding landscape, with islands, hidden coves and so much forest. As my eyes sweep over the slopes opposite, I notice a tiny cabin perched hundreds of meters above the lake, surrounded by grass and, most probably, planted terraces.

Baroso, the young and handsome boatman, starts

his motor again. It reeks of burnt oil and exhaust, and we continue our slow progress up the lake towards the waterfall we've set as our goal. Ernesto used his bargaining skills to get us the boat plus Baroso's services for 25 CUCs. Luckily, the battered metal vessel has a roof, an old piece of rippled plastic fixed to iron rods. The sun is getting stronger by the minute. There's an orange life jacket – just one – hanging from a rod. I drift into a heroic daydream about rescuing my companions: Julian can't swim and neither can Ernesto. The boat is filling with water as I deftly pull the life jacket over Julian's head and show Ernesto how to hang onto the boat, which is about to capsize. I'm going to swim for shore, pushing the capsized boat with a man dangling from each side. Oops – what about Baroso! Can he swim? My lifesaving fantasy gets too complicated and fades. Dream over.

Ernesto, Julian and I are sitting on the front bench of the boat, facing forward. Baroso has provided an old plastic tablecloth to shield our knees from the spray. With this added protection, the air feels warm and the sun makes us squint and smile. Ernesto chooses this moment to open the bag he mysteriously fished from the depths of his trunk as we were leaving the parking lot. Not a snack (as I had thought), but a bottle of rum, several cans of lemon soda and plastic cups. He pours rum and lemon drinks for us all; our boatman declines, possibly for safety reasons. When I take a sip, I feel the rum unslinging my muscles immediately, and decide one cup will be enough. Julian and Ernesto have two or three cups each and develop ever-broadening smiles as they admire the scenery and talk about *campesino* life in the mountains.

After an hour and a half, we reach the far end of the lake, where there's still a twenty-minute walk to the waterfall. Baroso, now sporting a dashing white Panama hat, drives the boat right up onto the shore, so that we can jump to a grassy bank from the prow. Ernesto debarks first and is thus able to steady Julian, who jumps awkwardly and falls forward onto the bank. "*Cuidado, hombre!*" exclaims Ernesto, as he pulls Julian to his feet and dusts off his trousers. It's slightly embarrassing, but everyone laughs it off.

We start our walk, leaving the rum and Baroso in the boat. The jungle is lovely – bird calls and flickering sunlight filtered through nodding leaves. We follow the mossy path, stepping over little brooks and raised tree roots. Except that Julian doesn't always do that; once or twice he steps right into the brook. I look at his wet feet in surprise. "Heh heh... I think I'm a little bit drunk," he apologizes. I think he is too, but don't want to acknowledge it.

Soon afterwards we can hear the waterfall. It's not the free-hanging curtain of water I imagined, but a strong stream gushing over a rockface from a great height. What's really spectacular is the water's clarity – one can see to the bottom of the emerald pools, which are several meters deep. Too bad I didn't wear a bathing suit under my clothes, I think. But then I notice the coating of fine mud on the rocks all around us, and wonder how I'd be able to pull myself out of the water without slipping back in. Ernesto notices the slippery surfaces too, and seats Julian on a stony ledge, out of harm's way. Alone with our natural wonder, we take photos of each other, posing carefully so as not to risk an involuntary dive.

Back at the boat again, we find Baroso chatting with a peasant woman and her son, a boy of about ten. They live in one of the mountain huts we've noticed from the boat and apparently spend their afternoons sitting at the head of the waterfall trail, hoping to collect a one CUC entrance fee from any foreign tourists who happen along. I give them a coin and wonder what they will do with the money. There can't be any shops for miles; maybe they have to give it to the government. I also wonder why the boy isn't in school. Maybe he'll have a boat like Baroso's some day.

We're chugging back along the other side of the lake now. Julian, who is downcast and quiet, flicks his plastic cup into the lake, as if to destroy the evidence. I am surprised at this careless act of pollution, but say nothing. Ernesto has stowed the rum out of sight and is basking in the sun on the prow. I am inwardly fuming at them both for nearly ruining the outing. Baroso steers us close to a sunny cliff face and points to a ledge, where he says there's a *maja de Santa Maria*. I'm not sure what that is, but Ernesto gets very excited and takes a small video camera from his jacket pocket. I ask Julian what a *maja* is. "A snake, a very big snake," he answers. Indeed it is; it's a Cuban boa, the largest species in the country. I begin to discern the dark patterned coils of the reptile as we draw within several feet of its ledge. It's as big around as my upper arm. Ernesto is now standing on the very tip of the prow, impatiently fumbling with his camera. The snake starts to uncoil with a liquid, unhurried motion.

"*Edder, me puede ayudar?*" calls Ernesto, almost begging me for help. He can't work the camera. I'm no expert, but I reach out and give it a try, pushing buttons, shading my eyes in the bright sunlight to see if it's recording. The snake, now uncoiled, starts gliding along the ledge.

"*Lo siento, Ernesto, pero no puede operarlo.*" I feel terrible that I can't get his camera to work either. And time is getting short. The boa is getting away and I want to try a shot with my camera. Shaky, I step out onto the prow to get a better view of the reptile. I manage two or three photos as it slithers along the ledge to its refuge in the rock. Ernesto is mute with despondence. A six– to eight-foot Cuban boa and he hasn't got a record of it. I promise to send him a print, but it's clearly not as good as a video in his eyes.

Back near our starting point, Ernesto and I are standing in front of a peasant's cabin four hundred feet above the lake, waiting for lunch. Chickens and turkeys and a lone goat approach us to see if we've got anything for them to eat. Ernesto is obviously fond of animals and used to touching them. He scratches the goat between its ears. "*Capra,*" he says, beaming, to remind me of a word I learned with him. But we can communicate in more than one-word sentences now.

"I'm at home in the mountains," he says. "I'm really a *campesino* at heart. I was born on a small farm, but my parents moved to Santa Clara when I was a boy." I notice for the first time that he is wearing flip-flops, and that he has walked all the way up to this spot on the mountain in them.

The water is almost royal blue from up here. Across the lake, the only hotel – the Russian-built Hotel Hanabanilla – rears its graceless head.

Baroso promised us a *campesino* meal for three CUCs each after the boat trip, so here we are, the only guests at Marta's cabin, waiting for her to cook our meal of fried lake trout, rice and vegetables. Julian has decided that he was strongly affected by the rum because he hadn't eaten breakfast, which is a valid hypothesis. So now he needs food as a remedy – and the sooner the better.

Instead of staying on the front terrace with Ernesto and Julian, I take a walk around the cabin, passing the open kitchen, where another woman is helping Marta with the preparations. Baroso, more boy-like in this setting, is leaning against the doorway, joking and laughing with them; he will eat here "on the house." The three of them seem to enjoy having work to do. Maybe they don't get customers every day. Marta, a cheerful woman in her forties, wears a headscarf and a big apron. She's a very good businesswoman, according to Ernesto, who comes over to ask her how the trout were caught.

I continue around to the back of the cabin and find the "toilet" – a small space enclosed by shoulder-high walls, open to the sky. Inside, there is a very clean porcelain toilet bowl with constantly running water – a hundred times cleaner than the lobby toilets of the Hanabanilla Hotel, which we visited before starting out.

A porcelain toilet is almost a miracle on this hillside without electricity, but being able to look into the kitchen while standing in the toilet is a little unnerving. However, the most surprising room in the cabin is the bedroom: a peek through the open window reveals that it's decorated with at least thirty baseball caps from all over the world. I imagine that previous guests have left them with Marta as a token of their appreciation. That, or else they died here.

When I get back to the front yard, where a table has been set for us, Julian is seated alone, tucking into a plate of tomato salad with plantain chips. By the time Ernesto and I sit down, he has cleaned his plate. This is not the Julian I know, who's always so gentlemanly. However, I put on a smiling face and talk about the snake with Ernesto. The view through the gnarled trees down to the lake really is lovely. It would have been a perfect day without the rum.

———————

On the drive back to Santa Clara, Julian falls into a profound sleep, slack of jaw and slouched over towards his side of the back seat. Ernesto's reaction is to unilaterally end the period of mourning for Chavez by playing his private selection of Cuban music on the taxi's sound system. This is either to lighten my mood, because he can see that I'm brooding, or so that I won't talk to him about the rum. I'm not mad at him. Yes, he did bring the rum, but he obviously meant it as an enhancement. And Julian happened to drink more of it than he could tolerate; he certainly didn't ask for it, but drank it out of politeness perhaps. So why am I ticked off at Julian? Is it because he disappointed my expectations? For some reason my mind's eye keeps going back to the plastic cup floating in the lake, like a tongue to a sore tooth.

Ernesto suddenly cuts the music and slows down. We're meeting a funeral procession that's making its way up the steep hill toward us. The coffin, completely covered in a heap of flowers, wreaths and bunches of greenery, rests on a two-wheeled cart pulled by a straining mule. Behind it, the grieving family slowly climbs, supported and followed by silent friends and neighbors. Some are crying, but what I notice most is the prevailing silence and the effort to get up the hill. When the procession is past, Ernesto resumes speed and music, but I feel different: I'm somehow cured of my anger.

By the time we're approaching Santa Clara, Julian is awake again. Ernesto drives straight to his own place on the outskirts of town, and invites us in to have a coffee with his family. He's become so much more than the taxi driver who took us to the north coast a short week ago. Over the past few days he's turned into a friend who shares adventures with us. We chat with him, eat with him and even accompany him on personal errands; he advises us, gets us the best deals and even complains for us when meals aren't perfect.

Ernesto lives on the outskirts of Santa Clara, where there's more room than in the center. His home is a compound of one-story buildings, with his house in the middle and his mother's next door. The houses are made entirely of concrete, each consisting of a row of rather dark rooms – a kitchen and two or three small bedrooms – with a veranda running along the front. Before we have coffee, he gives us a tour. First we visit his mother and exchange pleasantries. She's lying in bed, fully clothed, because she finds this warm, sunny day in March too cool for going outdoors. Julian is a natural for such visits, and chats amicably with the old lady, putting everyone in a good mood. Then Ernesto takes us outside and shows us his collection of tropical birds in small cages. They are like jewels in their iridescent feathers. He knows a lot about them, like which ones migrate to Florida in the summer and which ones nest in Cuba. He's planning to breed some, but has already had to let one go because it was too unhappy in captivity.

By the time we get back to the house, Ernesto's wife, his teenage son and their daughter are waiting on the veranda with coffee. The son is finishing high school and wants to study medicine. He obviously admires his father. Ernesto himself used to work as a school reading specialist before he turned to taxi driving to improve his income. His wife and daughter both work in daycare facilities, although the wife studied economics at university. It's a pity, but Marxist economists are no longer much in demand. We have a simple conversation together and I feel genuinely welcome and at ease in their company.

———————— ··• ————————

That evening I sit in my room at the *hostal*, writing up the events of the day in my diary. I deeply regret my intolerant reaction to Julian's mistake with the rum. It really was just a harmless mistake and I blew it up out of all proportion. Seeing the funeral procession on the way home reset my priorities by reminding me that so many things are more important. I feel sorry I judged him so harshly. Seeing the plastic cup floating in the lake and knowing it would take a long time to disintegrate triggered an automatic, almost violent, reaction in me. I became intolerant. I lost sight of the fact that my friendship with Julian was just as rare as any protected species or environment, and just as important. He and I share a friendship that has overcome language and space and time; I can't allow misunderstandings and cultural differences to destroy it. I promise myself not to be so self-righteous and judgmental on our remaining excursions.

22
SANTA CLARA IN 2015

I T'S EIGHT IN THE MORNING and everybody's headed for work, school or market. Ernesto steers us through traffic chaos that would make a New Yorker's hair stand on end. A monster truck honking like a foghorn behind us, a bike just ahead to our right with a mini-skirted passenger sitting sideways over its back wheel, her knees encroaching into our lane. A pair of dogs out on a romp, crossing the street in front of the bike. Several other cars trying to merge into our lane from the left, and, on top of all that, schoolboys walking to school between the lanes of traffic, chatting nonchalantly, oblivious to all danger. I tell Ernesto he could drive a cab in New York City with no trouble, and he admits that Santa Clara traffic is starting to require his full attention.

March 2015 finds me in Cuba again, back in Santa Clara for another visit with Julian and his family. The two years since my last visit have held some loss and sadness: my father died in May 2013, and my mother has had two serious accidents, which has meant that I spend even more time visiting Canada than before. On a brighter note, my flat-mate Helga and I have started a project to walk the 800 kilometers of the Spanish *camino* from the French border to Santiago de Compostela, and have already done half of it. I've also started writing this book.

———————•••———————

When we're outside Santa Clara, Ernesto takes the six-lane *autopista* towards Havana. It's more or less empty, but the surface is badly in need of repair. He drives the whole way in the left-most passing lane, as this is the smoothest of the three, but even then he sometimes has to brake quickly and drive onto the grassy dividing strip in order to avoid huge potholes. We're headed for a crocodile farm in the Swamp of Zapata, which means at least an hour's drive.

Ordinarily, a croc farm would not be a high priority destination for me, but Julian and Ernesto think this one is not to be missed. I'm actually more into animals of a furry or feathered nature, but am trying to be flexible. At the entrance, Ernesto buys us three tickets at the lower price set for Cubans, which means I'm forced to speak Spanish the whole time. The first display consists of foot-long baby crocs so tightly packed in their small nursery basin that they constantly fight with each other. When really annoyed, they bite off each other's noses. The result is an abbreviated top jaw and a bottom jaw that looks like the sole of a pointed shoe. Not a pretty sight.

The next display features a three-foot baby crocodile, bound at tail and snout. I am given the poor animal to hold while its caretaker puts identical straw hats on me and the croc and then takes a photo with my camera. Result: a picture of me and the crocodile very obviously not wanting to be photographed.

We're here to see the big crocs though, so we move on to a vast, shallow lake, where dozens of the reptiles apparently live. Some of the huge beasts are in the water doing their log imitation, others are sleeping in the vegetation on the shore, and the rest – about twenty or thirty – are lined up behind a chain-link fence, waiting for a warden with a long pole to dangle fish over their heads so that they can snap at and ultimately catch the fish. The sound of croc jaws snapping shut – with or without the fish – is blood-curdling. At the same time, it's comforting to note that their timing isn't very good.

Just as I'm reflecting that one might stand a chance of escaping those jaws if one kept moving fast, a small group of Russian tourists push to the front and block our view. Right in front of me is a Rambo look-alike wearing a T-shirt that says in Russian: "Putin is my president." I briefly consider pushing him over the fence to test my fast-moving escape hypothesis.

At this point I hear a dull thud and all the Russians going "Oooh. Oooh." A shiny new iPhone has somehow been dropped into the compound. There lies the phone, face down, four feet from the nearest croc. The owner, who is very upset, wants to put her arm through a small hole in the lower fence to retrieve it, but the croc feeder vehemently advises against this. He obviously knows whereof he speaks. He goes off and comes back with another park attendant. The two of them march into the crocodile compound through a side gate, brandishing ten-foot poles with which they strike the ground or the occasional crocodile, to let it know who's boss. Despite this display of bravado, they keep a respectful distance from the reptiles. While they keep stonking the ground with their poles, the crocs begin to crawl off into the lake. This is when Ernesto reaches in through the aforementioned hole, grabs the phone and gallantly hands it back to the Russian lady, who rewards him with a big smile, although I can tell it's not sincere. Ernesto is everyone's hero for a few minutes; I notice the Putin-fan sizing him up, probably wishing he'd had the guts to reach through the hole. Julian and I slap Ernesto on the back and tell him how brave he is, but I've had enough of crocodiles to last me a few years at least, so we decide to move on.

The croc-watching has given us all an appetite. After stopping at a friend's house, Ernesto finds us a very reasonable outdoor restaurant near the Bay of Pigs, where we are treated royally by the pretty waitress, who innocently reveals that she has never been farther than Cienfuegos – about sixty kilometers away – in her whole life. Such are traveling conditions in Cuba.

After lunch we make a short stop to watch people snorkeling in a vast underwater cave (*Cueva de pesces*) that is full of yellow, blue and turquoise tropical fish. I sit with my feet in the water and watch the fish flicker by. Like so many tourist attractions in Cuba, this one is little-known, sensationally beautiful – and free.

Once again, I'm staying with Teresita and José at *Hostal Casita*, but there have been major changes since my last visit. Two years previously, I was the only guest because they had just one guest room. Then President Raul Castro loosened restrictions on building, buying and selling real estate, so José had a new bedroom built over the garage and moved his sons up there. Now there are two guestrooms with bath, air conditioning and the rest, and *Hostal Casita* is listed on Trip Advisor, where Teresita's meals are praised to the skies. What's more, the *hostal* is now always fully booked by tourists from Canada, Germany, Belgium and France, which means they're earning twice a Cuban doctor's monthly salary every night. Two years ago they could only be contacted by cell phone; now they have an email address. And further changes are on the drawing board: José wants to build more rooms upstairs so that he can convert all downstairs bedrooms to guestrooms, thereby doubling capacity again.

Things are looking up for Ernesto, too. With more private tourists at places like *Hostal Casita*, he has more clients and more income. He also has a brand-new granddaughter, whose existence makes him smile tenderly whenever he mentions her. A big family man, he's started taking his family – mother, wife, children and now granddaughter – to a rented house near the beach for one week in the hot month of August. Granted, it's a vacation on a shoestring, with neither restaurant visits nor new clothes, but they now look forward all year to spending that week together at the seaside. Ernesto's also extending his own house by adding a room at one end, so that his father, who seems to have alcohol problems, can live with them again. Ernesto has hired two workers for a week to help him build the room, so he goes home from our excursions to a full evening's work of mixing cement.

On one of our trips together, Ernesto announces that we're making a detour to change some money so that he can pay his two construction workers. We drive to the main intersection of Ranchuelo, a nearby town, where Ernesto beckons to a bling-covered young man with a shoulder bag, who is lounging on the far corner. The bejeweled money-changer saunters over to the driver's window and asks how much Ernesto wants to change. Ernesto wouldn't be Ernesto if he didn't first bargain with the guy before agreeing to a deal. He peels off some of the CUCs I paid him an hour earlier and receives a huge wad of Cuban pesos in exchange. They each count their money, nod a quick *adios* and we drive off. I'm amazed that the transaction occurred so publicly.

I turn to Julian, who is sitting next to me in the back seat, and say, "Was that just a black market exchange of pesos for CUCs that I witnessed?"

"Yes it was," he chuckles, "unfortunately Cubans are well-known for being up to their necks in corruption."

Julian is still teaching one of his English courses in a private adult education program organized by the Catholic diocese. His mother will be ninety-nine this year and needs more and more care, so Julian has had to curtail his working hours to spend the extra time with her. Shortly after my 2013 visit, he was invited to travel to Germany for two weeks to represent his church at an international meeting. He went, was hosted by a number of German families, heard Angela Merkel speak in person and totally enjoyed the trip.

His son, Gabriel, has definitively quit his translating job at the hospital to start a private internet-based scientific translation business with a friend. The internet is still not easy to access freely, but is increasingly available in certain parts of Santa Clara. His translation work is poorly paid by Western – but not by Cuban – standards. He tells me that, as the new political and economic relationship with the US looms, Cuban universities are scrambling to replace illegal copies of Microsoft software with free alternatives. "Everybody is learning Linux," he reports. Most weekly video entertainment in Cuba is also based on illegal digital copies of US and Latin American TV shows and movies, which are bought and sold each week and delivered on memory sticks. Here again, a Cuban move in favor of copyright observance is imminent.

Sadly, Magdalena did not live to see 2015. After my second stay with her, she moved to her daughter's, as she could no longer see well enough to live alone. We'd exchanged letters several times, but when Julian tried to phone her at her daughter's apartment last Mother's Day, he was told the sad news. She was a brave woman, who kept on living and protesting despite enormous loss. Her wonderfully situated apartment will no doubt have been sold or traded, since such transactions are now legal in Cuba.

In eight years of amateur Cuba-watching I've seen many aspects of Cuban life improve. For one thing, there's a very definite improvement in the material standard of living. More and better quality food is available to shoppers with CUCs; more meat is available and more people are aware of the importance of eating fruit and vegetables. In Santa Clara a huge and colorful open-air market is held on Sundays, at which everything – including the kitchen sink – is bought and sold. Imported goods, many of them from China, are also newly available in stores, things like washing machines and DVD players, shoes and clothes. On the other hand, government food subsidies appear to be declining, so that the poorest Cubans – those without access to CUCs – are still only scraping by.

Computers and cell phones are now regularly bought and sold, although there is still extremely limited internet access. Cuban cell phones can send and receive emails all over the world but are only linked to a local intranet, which can be monitored by the powers-that-be. Public Wi-Fi hotspots are however beginning to appear in Havana, Santiago and Santa Clara, although there is no private Wi-Fi.

Six years have passed since Raul Castro started reducing the number of workers on the state payroll. This, together with the boom in the tourist industry, has increased the proportion of non-state jobs to at least 25%. As a tourist with Cuban friends, I have observed this dramatic change with my own eyes: in the last eight years Julian, his son Gabriel, Ernesto and Teresita have all switched from working for the state to working privately. Only two of those four jobs are directly connected with tourism.

What hasn't yet happened is the unification of the two currencies, the Cuban peso and the CUC. Cuban economists have been talking about how to perform this trick without rampant inflation or a popular uprising for a number of years. The day has already been named – it's called *dia cero,* or day zero – but not the date. Yet if Cuba is going to re-enter the global economy, *dia cero* must come. A prerequisite for currency unification is higher salaries for the 75% of workers who are still in the state sector, which means the government faces the gargantuan task of raising money via higher taxes or higher tourist revenues.

This takes us back to the Cuban government and, ultimately, Cuban society. Among the most touching discoveries I've made about Cuba over the last eight years has been the widespread attitude of civic cooperation and concern for others. I've tried to illustrate this attitude by describing what I observed in bus, bank and cinema queues, and in a general willingness to help strangers in the street. What I haven't seen first-hand is that there's also an open-hearted desire among Cubans to help people in other parts of the world. Cuba has an estimated per capita GDP of $7,500, placing it near countries like Sri Lanka and Bosnia on the world income list. Yet unlike those countries, Cuba trains thousands of overseas medical students for free, and sends thousands of Cuban doctors abroad. There are currently 24,000 students from developing countries – all on full scholarships – studying health care in Cuba. Furthermore, for over ten years, Cuba has offered free eye examinations and eye operations to patients from all over Latin America under the program called Operation Miracle, which Julian mentioned to me several times. At present, the island has 50,000 health workers in sixty-six countries worldwide. Cuba was also among the first to respond to the World Health

Organization's call for help in the Ebola epidemic in West Africa: about 12,000 Cuban medical staff volunteered, many more than from either the US or Europe. It still astounds me that Cuban doctors stay in Cuba and earn $24 a month, when they could be earning high salaries in other countries.

The Cuban education system no doubt plays a role in forming attitudes by socializing children to volunteer and to feel solidarity with others. Back in 2008, when I was first confronted with the idea of Che Guevara's "new man" in the play we watched while touring central Cuba, I was highly skeptical that ordinary people would interrupt their lives and risk their well-being to help less fortunate foreigners. But in view of Cuba's record of providing volunteer medical help in international emergencies, I'm inclined to think there's really something to it.

The US-enforced embargo or boycott has clearly affected Cuban development and prosperity, especially after 1989, when Cuba lost all financial support with the collapse of the communist bloc. Austerity and isolation from suppliers have made Cubans masters in recycling. I've mentioned their innovative responses to shortage many times in this book. The upside of this can be seen in low-cost medical procedures or in public health measures, such as the mosquito monitors I discovered by talking to Magdalena. Such attainments are no doubt paying off against new challenges like the Zika virus.

Years of living on a shoestring have also led to Cuba's photogenic forms of transport, like cars from the 1950s, *bicitaxis* and horse-drawn *carretones*. But if the current rapprochement leads to normal trading relations with the rest of the world, Cuban innovation could easily be harnessed to produce cheap high-tech products, such as medications and solar panels for Latin America, and mobility products like motor scooters, simple buses and cars for domestic use.

Some of Cuba's achievements are the result of strong state control of citizens' lives; however this control is bought at a high price, namely the suppression of opinions that differ from or criticize government policy. The human rights of dissidents are not guaranteed, and therefore public dissent is dangerous, although perhaps not as life-threatening as we are led to believe. This is Cuba's Achilles heel; the country will never achieve its full potential unless the government trusts Cuban citizens to express criticism.

Cubans once again have freedom to worship as they choose, but religious groups are monitored, and proselytizing is prohibited. This is what I experienced personally at the Santa Clara airport when I was taken aside for cross-examination, under suspicion of being a missionary. Government attitudes towards religion may however be improving, as evidenced by Pope Francis' key role in the current rapprochement with the United States. Furthermore, the continuing popularity of *Santeria*, and the government's apparent acceptance of this development, is a sign that religiosity is a possibility for all Cubans.

Although my brief experience of package tourists confined to idyllic resorts seemed to indicate that the government was against free and open contact between Cubans and tourists, it is perfectly legal for tourists to hire cars and taxis and escape the beach ghetto. The possibility to travel freely as a private tourist, as well as the explosion of *hostals* and *casas particulares,* will ensure new and wider contact between Cubans and tourists from all over the world. This, in turn, may ultimately lead to a broader worldview for Cubans.

On another day Ernesto drives Julian and me to El Nicho, a trail-filled mountain park with lacey waterfalls. Guides have brought tourists to swim in the teal-blue pools, so the three of us sit on a bench, watching a series of cannonballs and belly-flops, straddles and swans by people from Montreal, Argentina and England. In this park, the tops of the trees are full of *tocororos*, which Ernesto never tires of pointing out to me, offering a steady shoulder for me to brace my elbow on when I snap the photo. With his new hiking boots, Julian is more positively disposed towards hiking in the forest. We walk all the trails we can find, pointing out birds and flowers and admiring the mountain views.

On our way back to Santa Clara, Julian, Ernesto and I again stop at a *campesino* restaurant for another home-cooked meal, one of many I've enjoyed with Ernesto, who is marvelously skilled at finding these places in the mountains. This time the farmer is a red-haired, freckled Cuban, who turns out to have studied economics in Moscow, only to come back to Cuba and take over his uncle's farm. He claims he can make as good a living here with his crops, animals and tiny restaurant as he could working in an office in Santa Clara. His house is at the top of a steep hill, so we can see many of his crops growing greenly below us. He has a big stand of bananas, fruit orchards, fields of grain and alfalfa, as well as cattle. A Cuban cowboy in a huge straw hat – probably a farmhand here – rides his tough little horse up the hill, leading a cow and her calf.

While waiting for our meal to be served, we sit at an outdoor table and just gaze, feeling grateful for the morning's discoveries, for the breeze and for our cold beer. Since it is our last outing for a while, I've given Ernesto a pair of bird-watching binoculars that I brought for him from Switzerland. He's very touched and has tears in his eyes as he takes them out of their case. He tries them out, exploring the distant mountains, the banana grove, the tops of nearby trees.

"Just like this is how I love to live," says Ernesto, who always claims he is a country boy at heart. "I don't need a lot of money or a big house – just my family and my friends and the beauty of the countryside."

"I'm satisfied with a simple life, too," says Julian, "except I would like to travel a little more – to see other places and meet other people."

"Mmm. Then you have to learn more foreign languages," counters Ernesto, "and that's very hard."

"Yes, that's true," answers Julian, "but the main thing to remember is that we're all human beings." Then, turning to me, he says in English, "You know, Heather, José Marti wrote that 'Patria es humanidad'; our fatherland – no, our homeland – is humanity. So we should feel at home wherever there are people."

"It's an inspiring thought," I reply, "and it's true of my life so far. Thanks to people like you and Ernesto."

Acknowledgments

A number of people helped me with this book when I was in dire need of feedback and advice. I would like to thank Cressida Downing for editorial coaching and moral support when the book was just hatching. Thanks also to Karyl Mueller Pringle and Jeannette Regan, who read and commented on the manuscript in its early stages, as well as to Jokelee Vanderkop and Miguel de Armas, who provided invaluable and detailed corrections of the English and Spanish, respectively. Finally, I would like to express unbounded gratitude to my first readers and biggest fans Helga Hillmer, Lydia Guldener and Monty Sufrin.

AUTHOR BIOGRAPHY

Heather Murray was born in Nova Scotia, Canada, but grew up in the United States, where she attended Harvard University. She has spent most of her adult life in Switzerland, lecturing at the universities of Bern and Zurich, training English teachers and doing research in applied linguistics. An avid traveler, Murray sometimes hikes or cycles long distances within the countries she visits. She first traveled to Cuba as part of her work, but has returned several times since to explore the country and meet its people.

74007472R00183

Made in the USA
San Bernardino, CA
11 April 2018